FORKS
In The
ROAD

SMALL TOWN LIVES
AND LESSONS

---❦---

JOHN SULLIVAN

authorHOUSE®

AuthorHouse™
1663 Liberty Drive
Bloomington, IN 47403
www.authorhouse.com
Phone: 1 (800) 839-8640

Published by AuthorHouse   05/05/2016

ISBN: 978-1-5049-6545-3 (sc)
ISBN: 978-1-5049-6547-7 (hc)
ISBN: 978-1-5049-6546-0 (e)

Library of Congress Control Number: 2015919907

Print information available on the last page.

CONTENTS

INTRODUCTION

By Lewis Turco

This is a book about neighbors written by a neighbor. John T. Sullivan, Jr., was born in 1947 in Oswego, New York. He graduated in 1964 from Oswego Catholic High school; one year later my family and I moved to town where I began to teach at the State University of New York College at Oswego.

John went on growing into his shoes while I began settling in at the College. After receiving his degrees at Syracuse University John married his wonderful wife, Charlotte, and began his family. When two of his four daughters were in high school our son, Christopher, dated the youngest, Julie, and John was elected Mayor of Oswego in 1988.

This introduction is not the first time John has asked me to write something – the first time he did he asked me to write an inauguration poem, which I was happy to do. I recited it at his ceremony. The One-hundred signed copies printed on parchment paper were distributed as keepsakes of the Inaugural, "...which," John wrote me, "still hopefully adorn the walls of many Oswegonians to this day (which at least mine is, and it is numbered 1)!" The poem was also published on paper in a broadside that was circulated widely:

OSWEGO

It lies in the curves of the lakeshore.
Across Ontario the last of the sun breathes light
out of the horizon, turning the clouds shades
of red to the west. The water darkens,
splits over the stones where the spiders live,
where the gulls alight to conceive of evening.

Hardwoods rise on country roads, their limbs
casting tall shadows into the silence deepening
among the tumescent milkweed and the cattails.
A twist of goldenrod runs into fields,
to the apple orchard fence where ravens
give voice to the dark quality of waiting.

The cries of geese are incipient
out of the north, over the great water, the turning
of another season. The thrust of wings, the high
call of flight before the changing wind, will
fall soon to Oswego's waters, send frog
and salmon deep, beyond ranges of color

that fades now as the light falls onto Ontario,
and a dream of summer settles along
the stone coast road like a fleet of waterbirds.

Subsequently, Mayor Sullivan proclaimed me honorary Poet Laureate of the City of Oswego.

Needless to say, I was deeply honored to be asked to contribute in this way, but John soon followed up by asking me to do a harder job: correct and revise the City of Oswego Charter as Secretary of the city Charter Revision Commission. I won't go into the particulars of all the grammatical, punctuational, and typographical errors one had to address, but they were legion.

John Sullivan was by far the best and most active mayor the City of Oswego has had while I have been a resident. He was instrumental in cleaning up the Lake Ontario waterfront which was a shambles when my family moved into town. Wright's Landing, the River Walk, the Town Hall center all were spruced up and turned into beautiful and livable environmental attractions.

Not least of these innovations was Harborfest, one of Charlotte's pet projects. It was not many seasons before this festival was attracting enormous crowds to town during the summer, and it is still doing so. But all great mayoralties must come to an end.

John went on to become Executive Chairman of the State Democratic Party from 1995 to 1998; he was one of the founders of the Democratic Rural Conference. He served as Assistant Attorney General in charge of the Watertown office from 2003 to 2007, and then he accepted a position as Deputy Inspector General and counsel for legislative matters with the state Medicaid Inspector General's office, relocating to the Albany area where he lived in Saratoga Springs.

During all this time John Sullivan never lost touch with his Oswego roots. He visited town often, gave programs frequently (my wife Jean and I attended one at the town library in the spring of 2015). Just after the mayoral election in the fall of the same year John's picture appeared in The Palladium Times with the new Republican mayor, twenty-five- year-old Billy Barlowe! (Sometimes one suspects that John might carry this being a good neighbor a bit too far.) (Just kidding.)

John kept in touch also by writing essays and articles, including the profiles in this book for various and sundry periodicals in the Albany area and elsewhere, but particularly for Oswego's daily newspaper, The Palladium-Times. I don't need to say more because those who enter these pages, even if they are strangers, will soon feel as though they know the City of Oswego down to its roots and have themselves become neighbors of my dear friend, John T. Sullivan, Jr.

PREFACE

Life is full of choices. Sometimes we make the right one, and sometimes we take the wrong turn, and sometimes we have no real choice at all. My life as a youngster growing up in the neighborhood of Oswego we call the "Forks of the road' has been adventurous, richly rewarding, and challenging at times, and through it all, wherever I have gone, in whosoever's company I have been in, be they Presidents, Prime Ministers or paupers, I have always felt it helpful to remind my self of where I come from, and the values I learned delivering newspapers to most of the neighborhood as a kid. I may have spent 25 years living in a big house on West Fifth St., but I have never forgotten that I come from the

"Forks of the Road". So, when the editor of the Palladium times asked me if I had a name for the series of columns I was about to write, I thought long and hard, and decided to name it "Forks In The Road".

I decided to use the column to share some of my life's experience as a native son of Oswego who ventured out into the world, raised a family, embarked on a legal and political career, did a bit of traveling, met lots of interesting people, and learned a few things along the way.

The column came about as the result of an e mail I received from a fellow former Forks of the roader, J. B. Kelley Jr., who wrote to tell me how he and some of his contemporaries read and enjoyed discussing my recent musings, political and otherwise, which this newspaper has published from time to time. He suggested I write a column about some noted local denizens of Oswego, both past and present, and I thought, great idea, JB! I talked to the editor, she agreed, and thus, my column was born.

I have been writing a lot since retiring from public service, and I have continued to teach government at the college level, which keeps me vital. I am regular columnist now for the Albany Times Union as well as the Oswego Palladium Times.

I am especially glad for the opportunity to discourse on my hometown and its people. I grew up as part of the Pall-Times family. My dad was a linotype operator here for many years, and was always proud to note the he was the President of the International Typographical Union (The ITU). I delivered papers for the Pall for four years with one of the largest routes from West Fifth St. to Fifth. Avenue, Bridge and Cayuga St. north to the lake. I am sure that was one of the key factors in launching my political career when at the tender age of 23, I ran for First Ward County Legislator, and won, and as they say, the rest is history. And it is that history, the rich and vibrant history of Oswego and its people that I drew upon in writing these columns.

Several friends and column readers suggested that I put my columns together in book form, and I agreed. This book is a product of those suggestions.

JAMES G. GROSE

In the midst of increasing incivility in our current political discourse, when ad hominem attacks seem to be more the rule than the exception, there stands a monument to civil political and professional discourse. He has lived his whole life in Oswego, and is in many other ways an unsung hero in our midst. His name is James G. Grose, son of Oswego scion Weldon Grose and his wife Ethel, whose contributions to Oswego's music community were legendary. Their son, James G. has left his own very indelible mark on the Oswego legal and political community,and done so in his own inimitable fashion.

These days, "Jimmy Grose" as we fellow lawyers called him, is less occupied with trial preparation, and more occupied with caring for his special needs adult son Glenn, but even during the hectic days of Jimmy's legal career, he always found the time for Glenn. The kindness and civility, and patience he displayed in raising, along with his beloved wife Norah, a very special child, spilled over into his political and professional life.

If you ever had a discussion, or disagreement with Jim Grose, you never came away from it with any sense of him being a jerk. Jim was always a gentleman and a scholar in debating the issues, and as much as you may have vehemently disagreed, you always left the discussion on a note of good humor. You always left with a smile, and being eager for the next lively discussion.

In many ways, James G. Grose was a mentor to me in my young lawyer days. I tried my very first case against him in City court before another very wise Oswego patrician in the person of City Judge Thomas M. McGough. It was a case of petit larceny involving a round waisted fiftyish grandmother who was accused of shoplifting at the Big M Market. Her crime involved the theft of a pair of baby socks.

Not the most scintillating or sexy set of facts, but important, nonetheless. After a long trial, and jury deliberations that lasted late into the night, with many requests for the read back of testimony, we ended the case in a mistrial...a hung jury. They just couldn't bring themselves to convict this nice old lady, against whom the evidence had been neatly stacked and piled high by prosecutor Grose. His Herculean efforts notwithstanding, there was to be no conviction. The jury just could not bring themselves to pronounce this nice old lady guilty.

It was during that first trial that I learned the truth of the old law school maxim, "When the law is on your side pound the law. When the facts are on your side. Pound the facts. When nothing is on your side, pound the table!"

The testimony centered around where the defendant threw the socks out of her purse, as she ran from the store with the manager in hot pursuit. Did the socks land between the sidewalk and the curb? As the manager testified, or on the asphalt parking lot as another witness claimed. In truth, it mattered not, but the discrepancy in this testimony turned out to be my moment to say, "Aha!" and bang the table! Jim Grose never let me forget that one, and I never have, often using the anecdote to regale my students about the art of legal advocacy. It still stands out in my mind as a Jim Grose moment.

There were many more.

An argument with Jim Grose often involved the invocation of some classic metaphor from Greek mythology, or the halcyon days of the Roman Empire. Where did all these stories come from? A little known fact about Jim is that when you wanted to find the District Attorney when he had skipped away from the surveillance of even his most loyal secretary, all you needed to do was visit the Oswego public library. That was his hideout. He could remain hidden there for hours amidst stacks of books. Looking for the DA? Check the Classics section!

One of the lighter moments in my legal career came at the hands of James G. Grose as well. I had been to the Dentist before court one morning, and my mouth was frozen partly shut with ample amounts of Novocaine (an unusual occurrence for me). When my case was called before then City Judge Frank Klinger, I tried to address the District Attorney, but all that would come out of my mouth that morning was "Mitha..Mitha...Mittha Gwotthhh...we had a flea bargain already agreed to on this case!" Judge Klinger laughed so hard he had to remove himself from the bench, and could still be heard howling with laughter from his nearby court chamber. Apparently, my sudden inability to express myself in my normal basso profundo way, my complete loss of the ability to articulate a point, was more than mildly amusing to the regular cast of characters in City Court, even the court clerk Wanda Henderson almost literally laughed herself out of her chair.

There were many other amusing and memorable moments spent with James G. Grose. When music on hold was first being introduced on our law firm's new telephone system, Jim called, and refused to again be placed on hold, saying to the Secretary, "Look, just put the phone down on the desk and I'll sing "Melancholy Baby" to you!" That was his ardent sense of humor on display. That sense of humor sustained him and many of his fellow members of the bar through moments of professional challenge that were not always pleasant. He is and was the kind of person Maya Angelou had in mind when she said, ". People may not always remember what you said, or what you did, but they will always remember how you made them feel".

When it comes to Mr. James G. Grose, the answer to that question is "Like a million bucks!". He is the kind of character a community comes to love and to cherish, and Oswego is fortunate to count him as one of its outstanding citizens of durable longevity. When you see him on the street, tip your hat to him or nod your head and say, "Well done Mr. Grose, well done!" Oswego should be glad and proud to have a person like James G. Grose woven into the fabric of its community identity.

Bob and Helen Chetney

BOB AND HELEN CHETNEY

I first met Helen Hennessey Chetney when I was a teenage disc jockey for WOSC, and she was the secretary for the station. She, as it turned out, was a great friend of my next door neighbor, Julie Ann Doyle (Saloga), and her family had run a pharmacy on West Bridge St. for many years. It was our neighborhood drugstore, just like Gover's was our neighborhood department store.

Helen ran the radio station as if it were her own store, allowing her two bosses, Fred Maxon, Assistant Station Mamager and Jack Burgess, Station Manager, the illusion that they were in charge, when it was really Helen who was running the show. In those days, a frequent visitor to the office to see Helen was Palladium-Times ad salesman Bob Chetney. It was an interesting courtship to observe. They were both well into their thirties at the time, and neither had been married, and as it turns out, they were a great match for each other. They married in 1963 in St. Mary's Church, and went on to have three children, first, a girl who they named Mary Beth, then two boys, Robert Jr. and Brian. They bought a large house across the street from the Hospital on West Seventh St., and took in college kids as boarders. Two of my best friends, Jim DeGolyer and Steve Epstein lived there during their sophomore year at SUCO in 1965-66, so I was a frequent visitor to the Chetney house back then, and often invited to share a cool refreshment in their large screened in front porch on warm, late spring nights. Their friends Gene and Julie Saloga would often drop by, as would other friends like McGee Kelly Maniccia and John Holiday.

My first political job was to operate a sound truck for Bob's campaign for County Supervisor for the Third Ward. I remember chanting over and over into the microphone "Vote Row A all the way!" as I drove the truck around the Third ward on election day. I also promoted the re-election of Jim Musico as Alderman. He and Bob were both Republicans. Bob won, so did Jim, and Bob went on to become the first City Supervisor in many years to chair the County Board of Supervisors. He later left the Pall Times after he studied for and obtained a real estate license, and started his own Realty Agency in a building at the corner of West Fifth and Bridge which was home to the former Loescher Funeral parlor. My sister Maureen and her husband Paul lived there as newlyweds before they sold the building to Bob and Helen, and moved to 96 West Seneca St. So my connection with the Chetneys was frequent, friendly, and lots of fun.

Bob and I would team up every St. Patrick's day to do a live radio broadcast from the Ancient Order of Hibernians on Munn St. for over 15 years. We became the kind of "Bob and Ray", or "Click and Clack" of the local March 17th airwaves. Neither of us would touch a drop of drink before sign off time, which was at around 6:15 pm in March. WSGO was a daytime only radio station at 1440 on the AM dial. We used to kid about sounding like Hong Kong on the short wave had we departed from our abstemious pledge during the program. We certainly made up for it afterward, and I think as the day waned on, and I was upstairs in the broadcast room and Bob was downstairs near the bar, he may have had a pre sign off nip, or three.

Bob could just make you laugh. Our St. Patrick's day broadcast often featured the men of St. Mary's choir, with such luminaries as Billy Joyce, Francis Dehm, and Paul Murray. among many others stepping to the michrophone to belt out an Irish tune Bernadette McBrearty,

8

a nurse from Derry, in Northern Ireland would discuss the Irish troubles with me every year in her soft toned lilting voice, and we also interviewed by phone, annually, such Irish luminaries as Eamonn McGirr from Loudonville, owner of Eamonn's Irish pub, who wrote the hit Irish song, "Up went Nelson in old Dublin".

Bob hosted his own weekly Sunday Irish program on the station that became almost as popular as Nick Sterio's Italian American hour, Bob and Helen also became steadfast stalwarts of the Munn St, AOH club.

In addition to all of his Celtic activity, Bob became the Republican City Chairman, and the Republican County Election Commissioner for many years. He participated vicariously in many hundreds of elections, including Helen's election to his old seat on the County Legislature, after it was vacated by another Third Ward icon, John T. Donovan.

One thing was certain with Bob and Helen, if you went along with them for the ride, you were sure to have smiles aplenty, laughs galore and lots of fun. So, in the spirit of St. Patrick, whose feast day we recently celebrated, "May the road continue to rise to meet you", Bob and Helen, and may your children and grandchildren be blessed with many many golden Irish memories. Bob and Helen, you were quite a pair.

Claude Broadwell

George "Buddy" Broadwell

THE BROADWELL FAMILY

I first met Claude Broadwell many years ago when I accompanied my dad on a Christmas tree buying adventure to his East Bridge St. tree lot. I would become acquainted with him again during my college years when I worked part time as a bartender at Wood's bar near the Forks of the road,. Claude bought the bar from George and Sarah Woods in the mid to late 60's. It was a working class neighborhood bar.

Claude was a kind of working class, neighborly, hardworking guy whose main job was at the NiMo steam plant. On the side, he sold Xmas trees, and he fixed and sold used appliances. With a lump sum settlement from a Worker's Compensation case and the proceeds from the sale of his East Bridge St. Property to Carroll's corporation(later Burger King), Claude was able to acquire "Woodsy's" and changed it's name to Broadwell's. He began catering to the college age crowd, expanded his square footage, and, as they say, the rest is history.

In the process of the next thirty years, Claude, together with his sons Buddy and Gary and daughter Diane, acquired several other "beer joints" as we used to call them, and ultimately wound up building an empire of hotels and restaurants which is second to none in Oswego, and are currently being managed by the next generation of Broadwell progeny, chiefly by Buddy's sons Shane and George, but still under the thumb of master builder of businesses George "Buddy" Broadwell. The new restaurant is named after Buddy and Cathy Broadwells bright and attractive young daughter, Alex.

Claude Broadwell became one of my father's (Sully-of Sully's diner fame) best friends. My father always called him "Hubie", a kind of acronym for a perjorative slight, as in "You be s--t!" I still don't know why they thought that was so funny, but they had many a laugh over that name and saying over the years.

I came to know not only Claude and his wife Sally, but his sons Buddy, Gary, and Joey, and daughters Diane and Sheila as well. They were great friends and good and industrious folks whose hard work paid off. Claude became my client as a lawyer, and he acquired Bayshore Grove and built the Old Timer's Inn, while Gary ran Broadwell's and Gary's and Diane built the Woodshed into a successful college bar at the Forks of the road. Buddy started the Captain's Lounge restaurant and built a hotel across the street, and eventually acquired the old Holiday Harbor, developed Steamer's bar and Grill, and now boasts ownership of Alex's on the water, a convention center, and two excellent waterfront hotel properties.

In addition, Bay Shore Grove became kind of the family compound and a successful wedding venue on the lake, and Sheila worked for Buddy as did Joey. It was always a family enterprise, and what the Broadwell's set out to do they did, and did well.

My friend Greg Smith reminded me of a conversation he once had with "Hubie" in which Greg asked him how he felt about all the businesses he had created and the success he had achieved, and Claude said that to him, the most important part of the success was his family. That was all that really mattered.

The Broadwell family is a great rags to riches success story. It is not without tragedy, such as the untimely demise of Claude's eldest son

Claude Jr., and some other setbacks as well, but those are overshadowed by success and accomplishments aplenty. The Broadwell's should be justifiably proud of the empire they have built. And along the way, Oswego has benefitted greatly as a result. Their two hotels along the river, with another riverfront hotel on the drawing board, are no small achievements. They run a first class operation, and they have helped to make Oswego a tourist type destination in ways that the Thomas Motor lodges would never have dreamed.

Sometimes, Claude's son Buddy can be a pretty hard charger, but his heart and vision are always in the right place, and he has a proven track record of success, which makes whatever he does a darn good bet. He is a hands on manager and entrepreneur who I am proud to call my friend of many years.

"Hubie" would be very proud of how his children and grandchildren have developed and nurtured what he began. And to think, it all started with a creaky, beer soaked floor, Forks of the road shot and a beer type joint with Genesee on tap, a couple of bowling machines, and a great juke box. From the humble acorn, the mighty oak tree does indeed grow. My hat is off to the Broadwell family for the success they have achieved, the contributions they have made to the community, and the pleasure of enjoying their good company along the way.

JOHN CONWAY

It is hard to believe that it was twenty years ago, February 2nd, 1994, when I lost my mentor, and Oswego lost one of its most distinguished citizens, in the person of John O'Connor Conway. John was laid to rest after a memorable mass and tribute at his home parish of St. Paul's. I was honored to be asked to deliver the eulogy, and courtesy of Dr. Lou Iorizzo, current Oswego historian. That eulogy is available on the Internet at http://oswegohistorian.org/2012/03/tribute-to-john-oc-conway/ for those who wish to read more about his life and times.

For me, the memory of having worked side by side with, and under the tutelage of a great man like John O'Connor Conway, is one that I value and deeply cherish. Those years left an indelible mark on me, and in many ways shaped the person I would and have become. His many accomplishments live on, and he is warmly remembered, especially during the gatherings of the Fitzgibbons clan, to whom he is forever connected, having married Mary Fitzgibbons Conway, known affectionately as "Meem". His spirit also endures in the person of his talented and definitive daughter Ellen Conway Kelly, and his twin grandchildren, Conway and Louise.

I first met Mary Fitzgibbons Conway when she was the school nurse at St. Mary's School. A trip to the nurses office there was always delightful, no matter the malady, given Mary's sunny disposition. She married John a bit later in life, and although he was twenty years her senior, that mattered little in their remarkable relationship, which was filled with joy, adventure, and a little politics thrown in. Their crowning joint achievement was the birth of their daughter Ellen on

March 9, 1965. Ellen's equestrian interests were a delight to both of them, and her decision to attend law school well after her graduation from St. Mary's in South Bend, Indiana (Notre Dame) was also a plus.

I won't repeat the stories here that I told in John's eulogy, as they are still available to read, but I will add a couple of new ones.

I was privileged to accompany John on many trips to Albany and elsewhere to attend state Democratic meetings. In addition to serving three terms as Mayor and as City Attorney for Mayor Ralph Shapiro, John was the Oswego County Democratic Chair for twenty years, from 1956 to 1976, when I succeeded him in that position.

I remember him telling me on the way to a meeting at the Dewitt Clinton hotel in Albany, that the first person we would see there at the corner of the bar would be Charlie Torch, and that he would be the last person we would see in the same spot when we left. Sure enough, John was right. Charlie was an attorney and a lobbyist for the Teamsters, and a kind of political hanger on type with big bug eyes and a hollow leg. He even ran for office once with his campaign slogan being, "Honesty is no substitute for experience!" Charlie Torch was a legendary character in Albany politics, and John knew him well. He also introduced me to Albany Mayor Erastus Corning, and legendary Albany County Chair Dan O'Connell. These names are familiar to any longtime Albany politicos and their legends are chronicled in William Kennedy's book "Oh, Albany!"

Thanks to John, I met many of them, and these acquaintances and the resultant stories I could tell served me well when I became State

Co- Chair of the party myself, spending lots of time in Albany and New York City.

When I ran for the Assembly in 1974, I think John was just as excited as I was about our prospects for victory. He would show up often at our campaign headquarters above Wayne's drug store, in s building he owned and "rented" gratis to the Democratic Party. We came close, but we didn't win, and John made sure I got appointed to a "session" job with the NYS Assembly after the loss. That job was a godsend for me and my growing family as I graduated law school that May, and commuted to Albany once a week by train. I earned enough money in that job that I didn't have to work during the summer, so I could study full time for the bar. I passed it, and then got a job working in John's law firm with Mike Shanley, and as they say, the rest is history.

I am forever grateful to John Conway for helping to lift me up by my bootstraps, and cheering me on my way in life. He was as good a friend as he was a boss. They just don't make them better than John Conway.

Actually, there are very few individuals left of John Conway's standing. He was a true gentleman, a lace curtain Irishman with a respect for those of us with more shanty backgrounds, Harvard educated, well mannered, and a man of more deeds than words. His memory lives on, his legacy endures, and his inspiration still lingers in the hearts of those who were blessed with the pleasure of his company.

THE CRISAFULLI FAMILY

As a kid growing up at the Forks of the road in the 1950's, I was very much aware of the ethnic enclaves that existed in Oswego, and the neighborhoods that were primarily Italian, Polish, or Irish. Those were the three biggest immigrant groups that comprised the bulk of 1950's Oswego.

Oswego was a very Catholic community, with seven Catholic churches, three Catholic elementary schools, and a new Catholic high school. Only one of those schools remains today, and the churches have been consolidated in large part, one lies fallow, and another was torn down (the French Canadian Church, St. Louis's) and replaced with a Credit Union office. OCHS may be gone., and the old St. Paul's church and St. Mary's School torn down, but the ethnic legacy of these institutions and the people who built them lives on.

Speaking of ethnic legacies. There are many Oswego families of Sicilian origin. there was a great diaspora from Sicily in the early 1900's. My late wife's grandfather, Gaetano Tesoriero, from Stromboli, was one of them. The Tesoriero name lives on, as do names like Canale, and Vona, and Crisafulli.

As I think about it, the name Crisafulli may even be Oswego's most famous Italian surname. There are lots of famous Oswegonians who bear that surname. I don't know how they are all related, but I am sure they are. I think of people like Alderman Anthony "Zinkeye" Crisafulli, and Catino "Tink "Crisafulli, and their progeny. I think of Tinks' son, the late Kenny Crisafulli, chef at the "other" Oswego

Country club on the East River road for many years, and his sister Ann, who is still working occasionally as a waitress at the famed Wade's diner, where they never write down your order, but simply commit it to memory.

And then there was John "Fuddy" Crisafulli, owner of Fuddy's Sporting Goods store, and aspiring Oswego politician. And the Crisafulli brother's importing business on East Fourth St.. They specialized in importing bananas and other tropical fruits.

And there were the East Fifth St. Crisafulli's. I have fond remembrances of Freddie's (Chef Freducci's) branch of the family. Fred, who I am happy to say I appointed as Oswego's first and only "Director of Tourism", is the sole survivor of that clan today, and he still proudly wears his navy uniform. The same blue type uniform that his brother Charles C. Crisafulli was wearing in February of 1942 when his ship, the USS Truxton, was sunk off the coast of Newfoundlad, making him the first American war fatality from Oswego. They named the Italian American War Veteran's post after him.

Fred still greets the Tourist vessels that dock in Oswego, as he has done for many years. We even equipped him with a bright yellow and blue tourist bus, replete with microphone, for narrated tours of the city. The bus has long since gone to rust, but Freddy is still shining on!

One of the most unique characters ever to run a business in Oswego was Fred's late brother Joseph H.("Joe") Crisafulli, who ran the 1850's house that Fred served as chef for. It was a unique, Greenwich village type combination antique shop, bar, and restaurant. Their veal ala 'francaise was out of this world, and the Fra Diavlo was to die for as well. It stood near the corner of East Fourth and Bridge Sts., and was decorated in a very elaborate way, with a grand piano at the heart of the dining oom for Joe to serenade customers with. I remember many a night spent there singing along with Joe, who was Oswego's version of the Man of LaMancha. A high school vocal music teacher who returned here from Long Island, he was a director and producer of many high school musicals, and often performed himself in productions at SUNY Oswego. He was a grand character indeed, and ably assisted, in addition to Fred, by his sister Marge and her husband Bill Mercier, who always had a good joke to tell, and Bill's laugh was just infectious.

I always admired a certain painting that hung on the wall at the 1850's house, and I used to try to buy it from Joe, every time I went there. He would never sell it. It became a running joke. After my wife died in 1999, Joe showed up at my house and handed me the painting. It is of a young boy guiding a donkey with his girlfriend riding on top. I don't know why, but I love that painting, and it is today one of my most valued possessions. It hangs proudly on my wall even now.

I guess what I love is the contributions to the community that the Crisafulli family have made and continue to make to this day. They are a talented, fun loving, smart,clever, and active bunch. They brought their hearts over from Sicily, and pumped lots of wonderful life's blood into their newly adopted environment, and Oswego is indeed the better for it. Sicily's loss was Oswego's gain. So cheers, and' 'A salute" to all of the Oswego Crisafulli's. You're Oswego's Italian royalty to me!

John T. Sullivan Jr. and Charlotte M. Sullivan

CHARLOTTE MCQUEEN SULLIVAN

I am always glad to hear from readers of this column with suggestions as to who I should write about next. I particularly appreciate the feedback of people like Marg Falise, who wrote me to say that, "other than the obits, it's great to look forward to such uplifting and nostalgic columns." I also heard from J. B. Kelly Jr., who suggested, among others, that I write about my late wife, Charlotte.

I had to give that a lot of thought. Obviously, it is hard for me to be objective in writing about her, but I thought, why not at least try? And with the 14th anniversary of her passing weighing heavily on my mind and spirits, I thought it might be a good exercise to share some stories about her, and her indomitable spirit, as we approach the holiday season.

Charlotte was a very determined, passionate person, who wore her heart on her sleeve. She is known for her magical smile, and it was magical. She was not always smiling, however. In private, she could be a tough taskmistress at times, and you always knew where she stood. We could be engaged in a fierce discussion about something, and the decibel levels of the conversation could be escalating, and the phone would ring, and she would say, cheerily, hello? And all the rancor would instantly melt. Sometimes I was happy for those interruptions.

I think the reason for her intensity was that somehow, she knew her time was limited, and she wanted to get as much done as possible. I remember her breaking down crying at the funeral of her good friend Rosalie Garno, who died way too young as well, and saying to me, I fear the same thing will happen to me. Sadly, a few years later, it did. The thing about Charlotte's illness though, was that it was transformational.

Most people would have pulled the covers up over their head and stayed in bed when they got the diagnosis the doctors gave her in October of 1997. But not Charlotte. We had flown to Boston for a third biopsy, since the first two were inconclusive, and she was growing weaker and sicker each day. Finally, we got the news, on October 21st, 1997, our 25th wedding anniversary. I will never forget being in a Supermarket in Boston, when I got the call to come back to the hospital. They had reached a diagnosis. At that very moment, the sound of Andy Williams singing the "Theme from Love story" came over the sound system, and my heart began to sink as I listened to the words:

"Where do I begin
To tell the story
Of how grateful love can be
The sweet love story
That is older than the sea
That sings the truth about the love she brings to me
Where do I start"

I hurried over to the hospital with my heart sinking in my chest just before we were given the verdict by the doctors. I stopped in the hospital chapel to pray before going up on the elevator to face the real music. The doctors told us that her illness was fatal, and that they could engage in "palliative" care, but that there was no cure, and it would be a matter of months. (It turned out to be 25 months). I don't think my heart has ever been as low before or after that day. They had put a shunt in her liver, and injected chemo into the tumor to necrotize it, and she was beginning to feel some relief. She was stoic about it, and just wanted to get out of the hospital and get home. I set up a conference call with the girls, and they all made the trek to Boston before she was discharged. It was a tough time. But then, she started getting better. She felt better. She looked better. You could hardly tell she had contracted a fatal disease, and she refused to be beaten by it. She was the strongest one of all of us in facing the future, and she decided to hold her head high, and to cherish every moment of life that the good Lord deigned to give her.

At a Celebration of Life organized by her friends, on December 8, 1997, 700 people showed up at Hewitt Union to cheer on her recovery, and pay tribute to her passion for life. As she spoke to the assembled crowd, she said, "I want to share with you that I couldn't be here tonight if it were not for all of your prayers. and all of your encouragement, and all of your love. I am such a blessed person that I have this kind of friendship. You know, in the movie, "It's a Wonderful life", when Jimmy Stewart was at his wits end when the angel came down, and then when everybody came down and supported him, and the angel left him his Tom Sawyer book with the inscription in it being, "You're never a failure if you have a friend. Well I feel I am a smashing success tonight because I have all of you. Thank you so much for being my friend". (You can actually see the video on Youtube at :https://www.youtube.com/watch?v=Rk8YaAh--m4).

That is the Charlotte I knew and loved, and the Charlotte the community came to appreciate and cherish. It is was her cheer and determination, in the face of insurmountable odds that inspired us all. That is her lasting gift to all of us. Never give up hope, and never stop believing in the goodness of others. That's not a bad holiday message for us all, come to think about it.

Left to Right row 1, Bill Mercier, Mayor Sullivan,
John Canale, row 2 Avery Johnson, Tom Halpin, Frank
Clavelli, Bob Bradshaw, row 3, Bob Riggio, Earl Gardner

THE UNCOMMON COUNCIL

During my campaign for Mayor in 1987, we decided to use the new technology of videotaping all campaign events, so that we could share them with viewers on the local cable channel. As a result, I have hundreds of hours of videotapes of campaign and other events that occurred during my administration (1988-91), forever ensconced on video tape, and recently, when I uncovered an old box of videotapes, I started reviewing some to see what might be transferred to DVD, donated to the City library, or even uploaded to Youtube. (Yes, the technology has come a long way since the shoulder held video cam with the luggage sized bag with arm strap).

As I reviewed some of these old tapes, memories started flooding back, and I thought, why not share a few of the highlights of my four year adventure presiding over the Common Council meetings in this column. Some of you might even remember the incidents about which I am going to write.

We had pretty good "Neilsen" ratings back in those days, as the first Mayoral administration to air the Common Council meetings on TV, videotaped, and then live, over the local cable channel. It became, for some, the <u>Monday night</u> follies.

At every meeting, we opened with a public comment session, which was broadcast, and lots of folks turned out to have their say, some serious, some serial critics. and some a little on the looney side. It got so bad at times that my wife refused to watch the program. She couldn't understand how or why I would want to put myself through all of that aggravation.

It wasn't easy, and I have to say that over four years, only once did I actually respond to one of my critics publicly. Mostly I smiled and simply endured the naysaying. I actually had a method of coping with it. You see, before each Council meeting, I would take a deep breath inside my office before walking out to the dais, and think to myself, "Gardol shield". I remember the Gardol commercial for Colgate toothpaste. (www.youtube.com/watch?v=QGCRh5o41Xo) It was supposed to give you a complete shield against the nasty Mr. Tooth decay, who was shown in TV commercials as a little devil with a pitchfork, bumping up against the Gardol shield..as in "Boing!" So I would mentally envelop myself in a Gardol shield on Common Council nights, and wander out to the Mayor's chair to be insulted and harangued. I would listen, smile and say thanks you Mr. X, next? And people would wonder how I could sit there and take it without responding. They didn't know I was protected by my Gardol shield.

Truthfully, I would also be thinking that my late mother was whispering to me from my left side saying, "Let it go, John", and my late father would be whispering to me from my right side saying "Get up and punch him in the face" Fortunately, my mother's side won, and I did not engage, and as a result, my frequent critics never got page one of the Pall Times, which they would have if I had responded. Occasionally, I would go home and let out a primal scream in the bathroom.

There was one exception. One night, a very well known Oswego landlord who was famous for not paying his taxes on time, showed up to speak out on some controversy of the day. I couldn't resist saying to Mr. X, with a broad smile, "Thank you for coming tonight, I thought perhaps you were here to pay your taxes". Needless to say, I took great joy from the enraged look on that person's face... a moment to remember.

Another time, I remember a colorful local character, who shall remain nameless, but whose nickname coincided with a yellow crescent shaped fruit, accusing me of "Giving away Oswego's 'birthwater'" in our negotiations with Onondaga County at the time, over use of the Oswego water intake tunnel. I suspect that person might have had a nip or two before showing up at the meeting.

Another frequent critic accused me of dyeing my hair (I was 42 at the time, and non gray). Actually, at 68, I am still doing pretty well in the non gray hair department, without the assistance of "Just for men".

One member of the Common Council who was a frequent critic at the time, Alderman John Canale, uttered some of the most memorable comments. On one occasion, he accused me of doing something that was illegal. "Ill - egal" he said, several times... "and I'm not talking about a sick bird"! I remember another exchange with Alderman Canale when I asked him why he was so consistently negative. "I'm not negative", he said, "I'm not negative!", to which I responded, and on the question before the body, how do you vote, Alderman? "No!", he emphatically stammered. "I rest my case", I said. Since then, Alderman Canale has mightily mellowed, and even has an alleyway named after him behind City Hall. Someone joked to me that it was always called "Short-cut alley" anyway. When I see John Canale today, he is very friendly and respectful, and tells me what a great Mayor I was. Time is indeed a great healer.

These are certainly moments to remember from a bygone era. And in case anyone is wondering, I still have my Gardol shield in the closet, just in case I ever need it again. You never know when Mr. Tooth decay will try to make a comeback.

Ann and Bill Cahill

"Eleanor D" fishing boat

BILL CAHILL

My predecessor as Mayor was a pipe smoking, affable Irishman, named Bill Cahill. He was first and foremost, a fisherman a, and fishermen cast a wide net in their endeavors to insure success, and that's exactly what Bill Cahill did. As a politician, Bill was kind of Reaganesque, he had a pretty sunny disposition, and was a little hard of hearing, which helped him to avoid criticism. Lots of it, Bill just didn't,hear, which was just as well. I don't remember ever hearing Bill say a bad thing about anyone. He got along with political friend and foe alike, and always looked to find common ground with the people he dealt with in city government.

Bill's personality was kind of laid back, and he was generally unpeturbable. He left most of the jousting in the Mayor's office to others, and he was ably served by his attractive, smart, determined and capable wife Ann, who always had her husband's back. They were and still are, wonderful partners for each other, in business, politics, and life. It was Ann who helped Billw ith the toughest calls, and her fierce loyalty to her husband served him well, indeed.

I can only remember one occasion when one of his critics got the best of him. I don't remember what the issue was, but it was a hot button one that got Alderman Tommy Halpin's pants all in a bunch, and he hurled some kind of epithet toward the Mayor, who bounded out of his seat on the dais, and took a swing at Alderman Halpin, who ducked, and the blow grazed the chin of Alderman Ed Matott, who had a kind of bandy rooster physique, but he could take a knock or two, and he did. His attempt at peacemaking landed him a sore jaw, but a place in the history book as well, as one of the few Alderman actually injured in the line of duty.

As a Middle School Principal, Ed saw and broke up many more fights, But the Common Council me lee that Monday night in the early 80's was one for the record books.

Lots of good things happened when Bill Cahill was Mayor. It was under his administration that the west side swirl concentrator was built. Bill fought the demolition of the old Musico building, to no avail. It was demolished to make way for the sewer overflow facility, and the construction of the dual pipes alongg the riverbank to collect storm and sewer water, and over which, they built a walkway, later to be known as the West side linear park. The idea was embraced and expanded during the two administrations that followed, and we now have an east and west side linear park, running almost to the high dam. Those walkways opened up the riverfront vista in a remarkable way, and gave Oswego a distinctive waterfront urban ambiance that was to become the envy of many other communities. BilL Cahill deserves,!lot of credit for starting that process.

The Wright's landing docks and boat launching facilities were begun during the Fitzgibbons administration, and completed during the Cahill years. The Eleanor D, Bill's beloved fishing boat was retired from active duty as a commercial,fishing boat. Bill Cahill was to be the last commercial,fisherman on this side of Lake Ontario, and the boat was,moored next to his fish market for many years after that. That fish market was wildly popular, especially on Friday's during Lent, when the line would stretch outside the door. Bill and Ann built a deck on the back of the building, for folks to enjoy the view of the river while eating thie fresh fish sandwiches. It was later exchanged and enhanced when Peter Coleman bought the building and converted,it into a waterside Irish pub. Today, the building is falling into disrepair, and it would be a terrible shame to lose this big part of Oswego's waterfront heritage. I hope the Mayor and City Council wiltake all steps necessary to preserve and redevelop the historic Cahill fish building, saving it's national historic character for generations to come. It would be a fitting tribute to the former Mayor, and 8 for one would join a chorus of supporters seeking to rename and retrofit thT historic structure, as a fitting tribute to the former Mayor.

As the old saying goes, "Feed a man a fish, and he lives another day. Teach a man how to fish, and he lives a lifetime. Bill Cahill taught lots,of us how to fish, and netted himself a proud legacy in the process.

Nick and Henrietta Sterio

NICK STERIOS

First there was Hi-Fi, then came stereo, and now we have Wi-Fi, Hi-Fi and stereo through Bluetooth. I guess that's called progress. Stereo sound is amazing because it has two sides to it. You hear the left and the right, and the blend in between.

I got thinking about the history of stereo, and as a former disc jockey, I lived through the progression of radio from monaural to stereo, from 45's to 33/13 LP's and from AM to FM, and then it hit me. When I was growing up, Oswego had two different kinds of Sterios. Big Nick and little Nick. One played a sax and led a band, while the other played records and made us listen to bands.

I am talking, of course about longtime Oswego orchestra leader Little Nick Sterio, who ran a men's clothing store for years, and on the side, served as a kind of local Lawrence Welk. Big Nick Sterio, was a beverage salesman and County Legislator who hosted a weekly Italian American hour on the local radio station, WOSC. Big Nick was big, very big, and little Nick was, and still is, little and short, thus their monikers fit, and as fate would have it, they were raised in the same household.

Big Nick Sterio, along with his wife Henrietta ("Hank") lived at the corner of West Seventh and Albany Streets, with their brood of 7 children. Nick was a sales rep for a liquor distributor, and was elected Supervisor and then County Legislator from Oswego's Fifth Ward. He served his constituents for over 17 years. He was very involved in the creation of the Oswego County Health Department. In fact, the

County Health Department building on Bunner St. today still bears his name. He was a proud Republican representative in the best sense of the word, in the glory days of Oswego's Republican Party and he served with distinction alongside such Legislative giants as Bob Chetney, Gene Saloga, and my predecessors from the First Ward, J.B. Kelly Jr., and Art Vincent.

He also was the sole person to broadcast live, and actually spin records from the downtown Oswego studio of WOSC, at the end of the Bridge, next to Spereno's Tailor shop, every Sunday. Big Nick hosted the Italian American hour, and featured music by the likes of Lou Monte, Al Martino, Connie Francis, Domenico Modungo and Jerry Vale. Nick was as fond of cigars as he was of saluting his listener's birthdays on the radio on Sunday. He was also a prominent personality in the annual live March of Dimes Tune Auction that the station would do every year, broadcasting live from the Oswego Elk's Club. That was always a big deal, and famous emcees like Phil Markert from Channel 9, would come to Oswego to moderate the program, which featured talents like Chickie Caruso on the accordion, and Joe Bosco and others from St. Mary's men's choir singing Irish songs.

In his later years, you could find often Nick pontificating from a barstool at the end of the bar at Vona's restaurant. Nick also made his own home made wine and his own home made sausage. I hear that both were "to die for". I enjoyed Big Nick's stories, his humor, and overall approach to life, if not his political persuasion. He and his wife Henrietta (Hank) had 7 children, four boys and three girls,Joanne, John, Nancy, Susan, Michael and Patrick. Nancy became the City Clerk, Mike a policemen, and later a politician in his father's mold and a Town Judge, and John a fireman.

"Little Nick" Sterio was our choice to play at my Inaugural ball as mayor. There was none finer than Nick Sterio and his big band, back in the day. I remember we had his orchestra flanked on either side by two sailboarts that we hauled into the Armory to carry on the theme of "Sail with Sullivan" at the black tie ball. 700 people showed up on a snowy January night, dressed to the nines, to help us kick off the new administration, and Nick's band provided the music to dance to. And dance, we did.

Little Nick and his two sisters were raised by Big Nick's parents, Carmelina and Onofrio, after his own parents died very young. They wound up in an orphanage, briefly, until taken in by Big Nick's parents. They were cousins who became like brothers.

Little Nick was one of the most talented band leaders ever to play on the CNY music scene. He was also a very dapper dresser and purveyor of fine men's clothing. His wife Adele was the daughter of my barber, Johnny Stracuzzi, and they became the parents of two children, David and Judy. I have often bumped into Nick and Adele at Canale's when I visit Oswego, and it is great to see both of them still going strong.

Big Nick and Little Nick Sterio broadcast their own kinds of music, and enjoyed a wide audience of appreciative Oswegonians, who still savor the many memories the two Sterio boys created by whistling their own respective happy tunes. Now that's Italian!

Mary Dault Dowd

MARY DAULT DOWD

Very few individuals have had a more profound impact on such a wide array of Oswego community life than Mary Dault Dowd, who for many years was my neighbor and lived across the street from me at 55 W. Fifth St. Mary passed away at the tender age of 94, in 2009, and left behind a 94 year long citadel of achievements. She also left behind the appreciation of a community, and the adoration of many fans and friends, and the lilt of her Irish laughter is still echoing in the recesses of my memory banks, and will continue to as long as I am able to take breath. We were kindred spirits in many ways, and were born on the same day, February 27th. Mary preceded me by a few years, (32 to be exact) but we would always exchange birthday greetings on our mutual birthday, ann often had a chance to raise a glass in toast of one another on those, and many other occasions. Mary was a happy camper, who exuded positivity, even when her sight started declining in her later years, her smile never faded, and she could still sing like a nightingale on a summer eve. We always joined in singing Silent Night (Stille Nacht) in German together at Christmas parties, and were pretty good at belting out George M. Cohan medleys together as well. Mary brought a kind of Christmas spirit with her all year round, and she was always delightful company.

If it wasn't for Mary, we never would have moved to West Fifth St. I remember her calling shortly after Mrs. Emerick died in 1979, to say that she thought that 59 West Fifth St. would be the perfect house for our growing family. She was right, and I am forever glad I took her recommendation to heart and bought the house. We were neighbors for 26 years. My children loved her, the neighbors revered her, and the whole community respected her and her sizeable talent, business acumen, community spirit, and savvy business sense.

Mary had a remarkable memory and she seemed to remember everything and everybody. Her mind was a steel trap when it came to reminiscing. I always appreciated the stories she told me about my grandmother, Janie Smith Sullivan, and about her growing up in the Fifth ward.

Mary was a staunch Republican, but a Republican of the old school, inclusive type. She never ran for office herself, but she was influential in political circles, and served on three different Charter Commissions, two for the city and one for the County. She served as Vice Chair of the Charter Commission I headed, which successfully rewrote and saw to successful passage a new Oswego City Charter in 1976. It was in an old fashioned spirit of bi-partisan cooperation that we were able to succeed in overhauling the City Charter. We did it against all odds. Most Charter proposals go down to defeat at the polls or wind up in the political crosshairs. Not this one, and Mary helped see to that. If only there were more public minded citizens like Mary. The world would be a better place.

She also almost singlehandedly raised the money to renovate St. Mary's Church, served many years on the parish council, and served on the Oswego hospital board forever as well. Like my wife Charlotte, she was also named a Zonta Woman of the year, and she could have been named woman of the century if they had such an award.

My life is all the better for having experienced a friend and solid neighbor like Mary Dowd. Her spirit lives on in the lives she touched. She was a remarkable woman indeed.

(P.S. -A special note of thanks to Mary Lou Dement Dawson for inspiring this column.)

Dante Maniccia

Dante's Atlantic gas station

FORKS IN THE ROAD

When I was growing up on West Seneca St., near the Forks of the road, there was a very well identified and cohesive community of people who called themselves "Forks of the Roaders". They were woven into a loosely knit social fabric in which Wood's Tavern and Pullen's were focal points, and Dante Maniccia's Atlantic gas station was at the epicenter, with the horse trough fountain at the tip of the intersection. Bucklands Grill, the West End Diner, Hellards's gas station and Jack and Benny's diner rounded out the commercial establishments, and Mike's Barber shop was the focal point of political discourse.

Otis field was where we gathered to play sandlot baseball, and where the carnivals were located when they came to town. You could ride the Tilt -a-whirl, hop on the Ferris Wheel, and win a Cupie doll plaster of paris figurine all in one stop, and end the night with a Sully's Diner original Texas Hot! Those were the days indeed.

I remember sitting on my grandmother's porch on Bridge St. across from Wood's, when the Ringling Brothers Barnum and Bailey circus elephants paraded down the brick surface of West Bridge St., where the trolly tracks, paved over as they were, were still visible. I remember seeing the Big Top rising on the hill where Gould's race track had existed(now Romney Field House). I remember going to the circus and even going to the Freakshow to see the sword swallowing man and the bearded lady. All of this contributed to the panache of the period and place known as the Forks of the Road.

When you are 9 years old, and explore the world on the marvelous mechanism known as a red Raleigh two wheel bicycle with white sidewalls, a horn, and a mini headlight for night riding, you are on top of the world. But tires need air, and they occasionally pick up a nail and become flat, and that's where the expert mechanics at Dante's gas station came in. Mousey would patch your inner tube and never even charge for it, the guys at Dante's were always willing to help you out no matter how busy they might have been, and In times of trouble, nothing beat the compressed air pump at Dante's Atlantic station to keep those bike tires inflated to their 28 pps inch maximum.. The friendly Maniccia brothers, Dante, Mousey, Joey, always welcomed the neighborhood kids and we kind of hung out there and listened to the Maniccia brothers stories. Occasionally The other brothers Rocco and Leo would stop by as well. It was a true family business, and Dante was the kind of CEO of Manniccia brothers enterprises.

The Maniccias were a proud West Utica St. family whose roots go back, along with their next door neighbors, the Canale family, to Morolo, Italy.

The Maniccia boys became the heart and soul of the Forks of the road community. You could buy a peewee pop from their vending machine for 5 cents, and then ride your bike over to Cam Driscoll's store on Bridge St., and for 25 cents, buy giant sized Baby Ruth candy bar and three comic books with the covers removed. Such a bargain!

We built soap box cars to race on Turrill St. Hill, often 'tuning them up' at Dante's, and we would pogo stick and stilt walk around the block, and we built kankees and tree houses in the backyard under the cherry tree, with booby trapped entrances to ward off snoopy girls, held our own circuses under makeshift tents and went to shoot sling shot u nails at Rats in what we called Rat Valley (the open sewer then running from the partial sewage treatment plant at the foot of Schuyler St). It flowed into the breakwall area near the steam plant. We even went swimming in the polluted waters inside the breakwall, because it was warmer there than at Sheldon's beach.

Summer always brings back such fond memories for me of the people and places who shaped my youth. I think I earned my political spurs by delivering newspapers on one of the largest Pall Times routes which ran from West Eighth St. to Fifth avenue. Years later, I ran for County Legislator for the First Ward, and my Forks in the road neighborhood came in for me with flying colors. I guess it pays to deliver the papers on time, and to try not to skip anyone. The Forks in the road neighborhood was my foundation, and when I grew up to become Oswego's Mayor, I was proud of the fact that we found and restored that Forks of the road horse trough, a veritable icon of that period, and got the fountain flowing again in West Park.

It was a long way, back then, from 180 West Seneca St. To 59 West Fifth St, but I made it, thanks to lots of help along the way from folks like Dante Maniccia and his brothers who helped to show us what being neighborly was all about. And as Yogi Berra once famously said, "When you reach the Fork in the road, take it"!

I did, and it has been, and continues to be a phenomenal journey. As Jimmy Fallon says, "Thank you, Forks in the Road, for being my solid foundation".

And thank you Maniccia brothers for being an important part of that process.

OCHS

This month's column is not about a person, but about a place: Oswego Catholic High School.

Fifty years is a long time, unless of course you're a tree, which measures each new year of growth by rings. As human beings, we measure our years by the intensity of memory, and thankfully, as I look back over the fifty years that have passed since I marched down the aisle and across the stage of St. Francis Hall as a graduating senior, (Class of '64) while the buildings that once housed Oswego Catholic High School may be gone, the memories of my four years there are etched indelibly into the fabric of my soul.

It started out as a converted orphanage, with two buildings that included the school and a convent, occupied by the Sisters of St. Francis from the motherhouse on Court Street in Syracuse. They wore long black robes and starched penguin like head gear that would make Darth Vader look on with envy. Whoever designed this nun costume apparently had no regard for peripheral vision. It didn't matter anyway because most of the nuns had either x ray vision, since they could see right through you, or eyes in the back of their head so they could see what you were doing behind them, even as they wrote on the blackboard.

St. Francis Hall was a newly built structure originally consisting of only an auditorium stage and basketball court, but was later filled in by classrooms on its outer flanks. Those classrooms were brand spanking new compared to the drab stuffy rooms in Bishop's Hall, where the Principal and Vice principal were located. Everything was connected by either long hallways or a skyway to the convent building, which was always a thrilling experience to walk through.

When we passed classes in those hallways, we were expected to do so in silence, and single file, and student hall monitors could issue you a "demerit" if you broke the rules, which required you to stay after school in the "detention" room. Now that was a scene right out of "The Breakfast club" movie. The detainees were usually a motley crew of rebellious spirits or star struck lovers who were there for passing notes. We did't do texting back then. We actually wrote notes and folded them over and sent them through a series of couriers to their intended recipient, all the while risking demerits and detention if caught passing one.

I remember having one of my notes intercepted by a nun. It was greatly embarrassing. The outside of the note read: "To a sweet girl from a boob", and in the body of the note I confessed to acting like a jerk and sought my girlfriend's forgiveness by my abject confession of stupidity and callousness, and a very long winded apology. The object of that note eventually became my wife, and somehow, she managed to get the note back and keep it in her diary until her dying day. And you think text messages and e mails have staying power? A well crafted note can survive for even fifty years, but the memories of those notes live on forever. As do the memories of the basketball games in St. Francis Hall, and the red and white cheerleading squads, and the record hop dances after the games, and the magical mystery tour of the transformed and theme decorated St. Francis Hall for the senior prom. I remember the May Day Crownings, and the basement cafeteria, and Father Taylor (nicknamed Wild Bill) and Coach Naioti (Bluto) and Sister Edward Daniel ("You get your Every Week every week, and if you don't get your Every Week every week you get your Every week every other week")and Sister Edwin, (who looked like Grandpa Munster's sister), and Sister Judith ("It takes sowid knowidge to get to cowidge").

And many more.

I remember the pep rally in St. Francis hall on Nov. 22nd, 1963 which was interrupted by Father Eugene Yennock informing us that President Kennedy had been shot in Dallas and had just died. I remember the numbness I felt in that moment, and the immediate expressions of grief on the faces of my fellow classmates who walked dazedly out of the building into the bright fall sunshine. We came of age that day, and nothing would ever be the same again.

The buildings that once housed the school are no more. There is a senior living center,a nursing home, and a day care facility where they once stood. But the memories of being a student at Oswego Catholic High School, "bearing thy ideals" as the alma mater went, will truly last for a lifetime and beyond, because those ideals of hard work, responsibility, and Christian charity are worth remembering and valuing. As the words of the alma mater go "clearly thy praises from our voices peal ". And, so be it.

Clark Morrison

CLARK MORRISON

A community, to be a cohesive one, needs a good community based newspaper. A good community based newspaper needs a good editorial page. A good editorial page writer becomes the conscience of the community, and it can be said with certainty that Clark Morrison III (1922-2006) was all of that, and then some!

"Clarkie" Morrison, as he was known to friend and foe alike, was a man who had an opinion, and whose opinion mattered. Back in the day, when newspapers were newspapers, and you couldn't satisfy your itch for news by clicking on your smart phone, or watching one of any number of 24 hour cable news channels, the newspaper's editorial page was the first stop of many toward framing an informed judgment about the issues of the day. When Clark Morrison III was publisher and editor of the Oswego Palladium Times, that was a role he filled with great relish, and with a compelling command of persuasive, often poetic prose. Clark Morrison pontificated extremely well.

In those days, you glanced at the front page, and then went directly to the editorial page to see whose ox was being gored, or what matter mattered most, and Clark delivered on a daily basis. As a result, he was both feared and respected, but most of all, what he wrote was read.

I remember one editorial he wrote about a then Superintendent of Oswego Schools, "Whoa, Dr. Carnal!" (and Dr. Carnal didn't last long after that!) If "Clarkie" Morrison got on your case, you were toast. It was never a good idea to get in a fight with someone who ordered ink by the barrel, but occasionally, I did. I wrote letters to the editor to agree or disagree with him, and I know I gained his respect. He told me so. Coming from Clark, compliments were rare, so you just accepted them with gratitude. He actually told me years ago, "You write well, young man!" I cherished that compliment, and today, as I write

any number of columns on a variety of subjects, I always think, what would Clark have to say about this, and how would he say it? My style of writing was greatly influenced by Mr. Morrison, a blue blooded, third generation scion of a great newspaper publishing family. I remember the legacy of the Morrisons, the Leightons, and the Waterburys. Clark was the last lion of that bunch to roar, and his roar was indeed mighty.

I remember my father (who was a Linotype operator at the Pall for 40 years, and President of the typesetters union) talking at lunchtime about sitting across the bargaining table with Clark during union negotiations. He told a story about finding Clark's pay envelope once on a stairwell, and how he later used it as a trump card at the negotiating table. Clark had four children, and my father had three, and Clark was waxing on at the table about how hard it was to feed a family of four on his own salary. At that point, my father threw Clark's payslip on the table, along with his own, and said If you can't feed your family on what you're making, how do you expect us to feed our families on what we are earning by comparison? They got a big raise that year!

I took a leaf out of my dad's play book, and as a paperboy, I tried to organize a union for the paper carriers. We got a big increase in our per paper delivered wage from two cents to four cents that year, and then our organizing efforts subsided.

When Clark sold the Pall-Times to the Thompson newspaper chain in 1967, I remember my father saying that the whole world changed at the Pall after that. He was right. Clark continued on as publisher and editor for 13 more years but it was never quite the same. He eventually became a lion in winter, his roar muffled by the need to increase the corporate bottom line.

Rumor always had it that some of Clark's best editorials were written when a bottle of bourbon was close at hand. He wouldn't be the first writer who got fired up on fire water, nor would he be the last. He was a classic, in the true sense of the word. Deerfield academy and Colgate educated, tested by fire in the Navy in WWII, a par golfer and above par fly fisherman, writer, publisher, Port Authority board member, and Rockefeller type Republican all rolled into one. What a legacy he left for his four children and six grand kids who called him "Bompop". His wonderful wife Joan also left a legacy of community service when she passed on just a year or so ago, as well. The Morrisons enriched the life of their community and their spirit endures today in the many people whose lives they affected, and infected with a sense of civic duty and determination. Count me as one of their great admirers!

Bob and Sue Branshaw

BOB AND SUE BRANSHAW

Let me just say it. What's not to like about Bob and Sue Branshaw? They are both the salt of the earth and the cream of the crop. They are a delightful mix of musical talent and drugs, in a very healthy (and legal) way!. Bob is the longtime people's pharmacist who made Wayne's Drugs, a little known Newark, NY pharmacy, a household treasure throughout Oswego County. Wayne's World became Bob and Sue's world as they expanded their hometown pharmacy and friendly philosophy from Oswego to Fulton, then Mexico and Pulaski. Their drugstores became the top selling pharmacies in each locality, chain drugstores be damned! Why? The personal touch, and friendly, caring personality of Bob Branshaw somehow percolated through every store and employee. Put simply, they showed people they cared, and it worked.

Part of it is due to Bob's outgoing and empathic personality. He is always attuned to giving personal service to his customers, and even still compounds his own home remedies, like his green summer gel for all skinwise maladies that bedevil you during the course of a summer sting, sunburn, or just plain itch, that you somehow just can't scratch. I think if he names it and patents it, he would be well on his way to fame and fortune, but that's not his goal. His goal seems, above all else, to be of service to his customers, about whom he cares deeply, and that care is palpably evident.

They have finally embarked on a major facelift for Wayne's and Bob has long ago let go of managing his other three stores, and at least one of his kids has followed in his pharmaceutical footsteps. Jamie,

Bob and Sue's third son, is wildly successful in his own right, filling prescriptions for a host of institutional customers, and still playing a major part in the Wayne Drug company itself. The Branshaws were married in 1965, and are the proud parents of four children, and ten grandchildren. Their children were schooled at St. Mary's and OCHS and OHS. One son, David, has gone on to become a famous golf pro, and has ridden the pro golf circuit. The other son Robbie, is a landscaper in the Syracuse area, and their daughter Suzie lives with her husband Steve in the Baldwinsville area, and has pursued a career as a physical education teacher. Bob is a graduate of St. John's school, the proud Fifth ward parish that is no longer open, and has since merged with St. Mary's. He also graduated from OCHS in 1959, and that is where he met the love of his life, and his wife, Suzanne Chalone,from Fulton. Sue was a vocal music major, and is the long time director of music, and organist at St. Mary's parish in Oswego, and for many years, was the music teacher at St. Mary's. I have many fond memories of grammar school chorus performances, in which all of my children participated. They still sing the italian Christmas song they learned as second graders, "Tu shende d'al estella" at family Christmas gatherings. It was in Sue's classroom that my singer/songwriter daughter Elizabeth got her start and inspiration, and Sue has continued to be a mentor and an inspiration to dozens of musically inclined St. Mary's graduates today. She is a remarkable musician and worthy successor to the musical heritage of the late great James H. Lally, Choirmaster and choral director extraordinaire, who built St. Mary's Men's choir into a force to be reckoned with Diocese and statewide. She has done a remarkable job of expanding on that legacy, adapting and somehow remaining current and relevant, musically. With Sue, you never know, you may even hear "hip -hop" Christmas songs some year. The sky is the limit.

With Bob, what you see is what you get. He is the real deal, and an almost surreal kind of persona that if they were to cast a movie of his life, you would expect Jimmy Stewart to be playing the role of Bob Branshaw. I'm not sure who would be cast as Sue. How about Sally Fields?

When, and or if Bob and Sue will ever retire is an entirely open question. I suspect not. They are both too busy tending to the needs of their respective flocks, children and grandchildren, to ever slow down, and why should they?. They are the rocks upon which the fabric of any community are built, and they have made a huge difference in the lives of many Oswegonians, for which we will always be eternally grateful. Good luck with the new storefront, guys. Just don't ever change who you are, and all will be well. Oh, and one last prescription...don't ever let go of the "Downtown Mayor", Mike D'Amico, under your guidance, he has become an indispensible institution in his own right. It's all part of the family of Wayne's that Bob and Sue built. Bravo to them.

Gay and Alan Williams

GAY H. WILLIAMS

Gay Hollingsworth Williams has lived in the Town of Minetto for the vast part of her adult years. It is in Minetto that she and her husband, long time Minetto Town Judge and retired Minetto Fourth grade teacher, Alan, raised their three boys, in their renovated farm house with the chicken coop outback. It is from that farmhouse that many early morning hockey trips emanated, and many family gatherings and much celebrating occurred. That will soon end, as the Williams prepare to place their Minetto Farm house, and its many memories, on the selling block. They will be relocating permanently to their newly renovated summer home on the shores of Sodus Bay in Fair Haven. And they hope to spend at least part of the winter is the sunnier and warmer clime of Florida. They deserve to enjoy their Golden years.

The memories they will leave in Minetto are bittersweet. The hardest thing they have had to face is the loss of their handsome and dashing, and newly married young Navy pilot son, their middle child, Nate, in a tragic jet fighter crash in California, while on a Navy training mission. Nathan was entering the prime of life, at 28, and then, suddenly, he was taken in April 2012.

It still makes no sense, and leaves a gaping hole in both Al and Gay's hearts, which will never be filled. But, two years later, they are learning to cope and are rebounding from their devastating loss, and they are learning to navigate around it, and continue to take joy in the relationships they have with their other two incredibly accomplished boys, Jeff, and Seth. Jeff, who married a local Oswego girl, daughter of a doctor, who is now becoming a Doctor herself, has finished practicing law at one of the more prestigious law firms in New York City, and has relocated to Denver, Colorado, and new legal career adventures.Their son Seth, who smiles a lot,and is the musician of the family, lives in New York City, pursuing his own career objectives in the world of finance. The remaining brothers greatly enjoy each other's company, as evidenced by a recent sojourn together to New Orleans for some brotherly bonding and frivolity. All this while their mother was off gallivanting around Europe to places like Rome and Monte Carlo.

Gay will someday soon be ending her career as Oswego City Attorney, and joining the ranks of the permanent bridge playing class. Her mother, the late Dorothy Hirschey was a reknowned Bridge enthusiast, who lived in Watertown. Her husband Charles Hirschey, owned the Climax Manufacturing Company in Carthage, a paper and box manufacturing establishment that is still thriving today, and is run by Gay's half siblings.

Gay has had a long and varied legal career both in private practice and in public positions, as City Attorney, and as a Confidential law Assistant to former Supreme Court Judge Eugene F. (Pat) Sullivan Jr. She was my law partner for many years, and my City Attorney for four years, a job which she says she found most challenging, since I often tried to be my own city attorney as well as Mayor at times. I always valued her wise counsel, even if I didn't take her advice from time to time. Usually I was the worst for ignoring it. Not content to simply practice law, she has served on the Board of the Oswego City library, and the Harborfest Board of Directors as well, where she contributed mightily to both organizations.

She also had a long and successful career as a pat time business professor at SUNY Oswego, following in the footsteps of her one time law partner Dennis Hawthorne.

My association with Gay dates back to our law school days, when we shared the commute from Oswego to Syracuse law school, often with another fellow student, Sue Zagame, whose husband ran against me for State Assembly, and won. That made for some interesting commuting conversations! She was always an ardent Democrat, even when she work for Pat Sullivan. She still is.

Gay was raised by a single divorced mother, who later married a wealthy Industrialist. She has a sister Lee who lives in Watertown, and is a legal secretary.

Al's pedigree includes being the son of a prominent Episcopalian cleric from Watertown, and the two married after Gay left Skidmore College in Saratoga, and Al left the Navy, after graduating from Hobart College in Geneva, and the couple moved to Oswego where they both finished their college educations, with Al getting his masters degree and going on to teach in Minetto, and Gay, graduating, then going to law school, and becoming an attorney.

When the boys were born, it was Alan who took a paternity leave to raise them, while Gay stayed working as a law clerk. It was a question of economics, (Gay's job paid more) and was somewhat rare in those days, but Alan proved to be not only a superb, devoted, capable and caring father, but his teaching and mentoring skills became even more finely honed when he returned to the classroom as the boys entered school. Those years when they lived in an apartment in the big old house at the Corner of West Fifth and Seneca Streets (the

Peebles mansion) are still fresh in my memory, as are the many years we shared social and professional experiences. I have many stories to tell, and some are even printable! Time and space here does not permit, but one favorite story involves Gay and Alan and Charlotte and I going to a fancy Finger lakes bed and breakfast, and somehow Charlotte made sure that the Williams got the servants quarters adjacent to ours. We laughed a lot about that.

In fact, we have laughed a lot about many things over the years, including Gay's propensity to "boogey down" hard at dances, and our shared enthusiasm for an occasional (or more) glass of wine.

Gay Hollingsworh Williams is many things. She is a devoted mother to her sons, a talented and capable attorney, and devoted wife. I can't attest to her bridge playing skills as I don't share that avocation, but if Gay is as committed in her bridge playing as she is in everything else she does, watch out Central New York and Florida bridge playing world, a powerful force is about to become more powerful as the retirement years approach. For Gay Hollingsworth Williams, there is no such thing as a Bridge too far to cross.

Doris with 1952 Mayor Frank L. Gould
and City Council

DORIS ALLEN

When I was a senior in high school, I took part in the Senior play, cast as the Headmaster of a Sleepy Hollow boarding school. I was cast opposite Liz Allen, the valedictorian of our class who played the headmistress of a neighboring all girls school.. The play was called Mr. Crane of Sleepy Hollow, and was ably directed by Drama coach Mrs. Doris Allen, Liz's mom. The Allens lived in a large Victorian style home on West Eighth St., in Oswego, just off Bridge St. Mrs. Allen was an extraordinarily talented woman with a passion for teaching and acting and directing, and of course, politics as well.

Doris Brown (her maiden name) grew up on a farm in Redfield, and later attended the Oswego Normal,school., where she was a standout student, and class leader.

She was the first woman ever elected as an Alderman for the City of Oswego, in 1952. She almost singlehandedly helped to insure the construction of Hamilton Homes, the first Public low cost housing project in Oswego. Opposition in the Landlord community was so fierce that she actually needed a body guard to escort her out of City Hall amid catcalls from an unruly group of landlords, who jeered and even spat at her after one city hall meeting. Her dad was her escort that night. He was a rugged, if elderly at the time, farmer from Redfield who was fiercely protective of his daughter Doris, and he landed the first punch on the offending landlord, which knocked him silly. There is a riveting account of the incident in the Pall times archives.Doris dabbled in lots of things and whatever she dabbled in she dabbled with gusto and enthusiasm.

Doris married Edwin M. "Jiggs" Allen, who was the business manager for the Waterbury family owned Oswego Palladium Times. Jiggs was also a politician, and became the first Executive Assistant to Mayor Ralph Shapiro and later John O'C. Conway. He was a brilliant strategist. My father, who was a Linotype operator at the Psll Times, always told me that Jiggs Allen was one of the smartest men he ever met. He was a colonel in the Army Reserve, and spent many summers in brush up training at Camp Drum. He was a man of many talents, and Doris was devoted to him and her three brilliant children, as well as to her career as a teacher, principal, and author.

Her two daughters Liz and Phyllis both attended Vassar, and later obtained graduate degrees, while her son John went to Cornell and Temple School of law, and is a partner in th e well known Bond Schoeneck and King law firm,. John opened their Oswego office, and still practices there from time to time today John reminisced with me recently about his mom, "She entered Oswego State Normal in 1938 which originally was 2 years. Her class was the first class to get a Baccalaureate Degree as the College went to a 4 year program and she was a member of that Class of 1942. Always active, as recorded in Dorothy Rodger's history of the College, she was in the President's Office when the word came thru that the College could offer baccalaureate degrees! She was the editor of the Oswegonian which has always been printed by the Pal Times. She met my father E. M. "Jiggs" Allen there." he added. And, as they say, the rest is history!

She became principal of the Number 2 school on Mitchell St., and later was the founder of the Oswego Head start program, long before Pre-K education was fashionable.

Doris has a passion for theatre and for bridge,. She is one of the longest tenured members of the Oswego players and has participated in many of their shows as both an actor and director over the years. She is an ardent and lifelong Democrat, which is another reason I so greatly admire her, and she was even a delegate,to the Democratic National Convention in 1976 supporting Jimmy Carter.

Doris still gives bridge lessons where she now lives at Springbrook at Seneca Hill just outside of Oswego. I am sure she would love hearing from her many friends and fans. Count me as one of them! (Doris passed away several months ago, and I received a wonderful, heartfelt note from her daughter and my classmate, Liz, which said, "Thank you so much for the article in the Pall Times about my mother. Mom needed accolades in order to believe that she had a right to exist, and you gave her applause when she needed it most. You praised her past accomplishments and gave her present meaning and life. Your words gave her dignity when she needed it most, when she was at her most vulnerable, betrayed by her body and longing to be sixteen all over again. I am in debt for giving my mother what she needed above all else...public acknowledgment...Fondly, Liz Allen Cody.

That is one of the nicest notes I have ever received, and it gives me strength to keep on writing about people who have done so much in their lives.

Fred and Norma Bartle

NORMA ADAMS BARTLE

Norma Bartle was a trailblazer. She was a brilliant woman who lived life fully and embraced opportunities when they came to her. She rose to each occasion with determination and good humor, and always had a way of smiling, even in her darkest hours. Hers was a warm, e Ingratiating smile. The kind that puts you at ease, and makes you think that if she is ok with things as they are then things must new pretty well ok generally. You could feel her warmth and generosity of spirit, and on top of al of that, she was a fun person to be with.

Norma was born in New Jersey, and lived in New York City and Albany before relocating to Fulton, New York at an early age. She was active in school, and was President of her Fulton high school graduating class She married young and became a mother at the tender age of 19. College was then out of the question. Her son Robert grew up to be a strapping and talented lad, but her marriage did not survive.

Things changed in her life when she met a young political science professor named Fred Bartle. In 1961. They fell in love while he was a graduate student at SU, and she was a secretary In the department. They moved to Minetto and bought an old farm house on the Granby-Minetto road, and set about restoring it to its former semi glory. Fred taught political,science to large lecture halls of eager young students in newly minted mega classrooms at SUNY Oswego, which was transforming from a Teacher's college to a multi-dimensional liberal arts education center. Norma involved herself in faculty wives groups, and was a founder of the Oswego Valley League of Women voters, where she met such notables to be as Muriel Allerton, later Mayor of Fulton, and Patti McGill Peterson, later President of Wells College, and St. Lawrence University.

Norma would often host small get togethers with Fred's students, who the Bartles would welcome to their farm home for cocktaills and hors d'ouerves. (The drinking age back then was 18, so it was ok for freshmen to have a glass of beer or wine). She would invite other townspeople and faculty, and would make sure the students felt welcomed, and were given a chance to mix and mingle, and Norma became the kind of Pearl Mesta of faculty-student gatherings at Oswego State, and the students loved her.

That is how I first met Norma, at a Fall end of semester party at their first Minetto house. They went on to build two other new houses on the same parcel of land, They were always building, adding, and changing.

Fred was the kind of Professor who loved to foster debate in his classroom. He was tolerant of all views, but you always knew where Fred stood, and his insightful manner and didactic lecturing style, coupled with his encyclopedic knowledge of all things political was an amazement to me. I wasn't his best student. In fact, the first grade I got in his class was a C. I went on to get straight A's in poly sci thereafter, but I have never let Fred forget that his humbling assessment of me in my freshman year was a wake up call that I heard loudly and clearly. He made you think, and think critically, and he was always willing to play devil's advocate with you, if he thought you were getting too clever by half. Fred was an outstanding teacher, and a great a professor, but he was more than that. He and Norma befriended many students and made them feel as though Ithey mattered.

Ken Auletta, author, former Newsday columnist, and New Yorker columnist was one of Fred's more accomplished political trainees. Dick Faerfaglis was another. Dick went on to serve four different Speakers of the NYS Assembly as political,director, and brought in a whole generation of Oswego interns into the real world of Albany politics. Dick got that job after managing my close, but unsuccessful campaign for the NYS Assembly in 1974. Fred was my campaign speechwriter, and Norma was my best volunteer.

Several years earlier, in 1972. I cajoled Norma into running with me as a delegate pledged to George McGovern in the Democratic Presidential primary. We attended the Democratic National convention in Miami, and had an incredible time there, even though McGovern's "Come home America" speech at 4 am fell on deaf ears and was seen by few Americans. It was a thrilling opportunity to be involved in politics at the national level, and it whetted her appetite for more, so she ran and won a seat from Minetto on the Oswego County Legislature, and became the first woman ever to do so. She then decided to mount a campaign for Congress in 1976. And again in 1978. Nearly unseating an entrenched Republican congressman, Bob McEwen from Ogdensburg.

Norma's 1976 campaign was the most energetic and exciting Congressional race the North Country had ever seen. She lost, but she won many admirers. She later served as regional representative for Governor Hugh Carey, and later Mario Cuomo, and traveled. extensively throughout the region, winning friends wherever she went. Norma's tall white boots and her long pony tail hair became familiar sights to thousands of Central and Northern New Yorkers.

One little known fact about Norma is that in her first campaign, singer Harry Chapin performed at a benefit concert for her in Plattsburgh, a few years before his untimely death in a car crash on Long Island in 1981. Rumor has it that he wrote the song "A better place to be" (which mentions Watertown, NY,) while on the campaign trial for Norma Bartle in the North Country.

Fred and Norma (who Fred affectionately called Normeo) built a much bigger farmstyle house, and then sold it and built.a more modern one on part of the same Minetto property. We spent many a summer afternoon there swimming in her new pool, and enjoying the company of her two teenaged daughters, Susan and Gamin.

After retiring to Charlottesville VA., the Bartles built three more new houses, Norma became a personal assistant to a multi billionaire philanthropist, and Fred became a docent at Jefferson's home, Monticello. In their later years" they moved to Albany to be closer to their daughter Susan and two of their grandchildren,Tim and Abbey Perry of Albany. Another granddaughter, Lisa Longley lives in Charleston, S.C.

Fred still lives near Susan in quiet retirement. Norma passed away this December at the age of 85, after several years of declining health. A memorial service for Norma is being planned for Oswego this Spring,

My memories of those Minetto years are crisp and filled with many pleasantries. Norma Bartle was a remarkable woman, a quiet trailblazer, a wonderful mother, wife and grandmother, and in these days when they say if you want a friend in politics get a dog, she was even rarer. She was a true friend. They don't make them any better than Norma Adams Bartle.

Bob McManus

Bob McManus as Santa Claus

THE REAL SANTA CLAUS

Every year at this time, many of us engage in a search for the true meaning of the holidays. That true spirit is often elusive to find, but if any one ever found it and expressed it, time and again, especially at Christmas time, that person was Bob McManus, the best Santa Claus Oswego ever had.

Bob was a business agent for Laborer's Local 214. Short, stocky, and always cheerful, at Christmas time, he would transform into Santa Claus, in the most believable way. His shaky voice, and portly demeanor warmed the hearts of many starry eyed children, and he was a frequent visitor to area schools, nursing homes, and family homes that invited him to get a taste of what the real joy of Christmas was all about.

The Sullivan family was one of those that Bob visited every year, and we have many special Christmas videos of Bob, sitting in our "Santa chair", near the Christmas tree in the front room of our large West Fifth St. home, enchanting not only our children, but the entire neighborhood, and the children of our friends who would come for the special occasion of Santa's annual visit, replete with Jingle Bells, hearty Ho Ho Ho's and his famous admonition to the children that "It's not the things you do at Christmas, but the Christmas things you do all year round" that really matter.

Perhaps Bob's quintessential moment came in the year 1988, when he was helicoptered in to the soon to be City Hall Plaza by the Sheriff's Department helicopter, and then the Fire Department's fire truck, to the stage in front of City Hall, as he wandered through the record crowd of 9,000 or so revelers and carolers who had gathered for Oswego's First Annual Children's Christmas Tree Lighting at City Hall. There was a 40 foot Colorado spruce, erected by the DPW for the occasion, a menorah lighting the steps of the old Post Office, and a chorus of children from all the elementary schools in the city, led by Leighton elementary vocal music teacher Sue Swindells, who stood on a box above the crowd to lead all the caroling. The high school cheerleaders provided Santa a cheering escort, while the Policemen's wives poured hot chocolate for the thousands of celebratory citizens in the rotunda of City Hall.

The photo which appears here, taken by Pall Times photographer Harrison Wilde, says it all. It was indeed a special moment in time. Alcan provided the Aluminum foil for the children to fashion their own ornaments in their art classes, which the DPW then hung high on the City Christmas tree. Little children hung their own ornaments from the reachable parts of the bottom of the tree, while Nestle provided the free hot chocolate. I remember one Syracuse TV channel newsman saying it was like a scene out of a Norman Rockwell painting, that first Children's Christmas Tree lighting at City Hall Plaza, and the standout performer who enchanted all from the stage was Oswego's own Santa, Bob McManus.

Sadly, it was a mere one year later that we lost Oswego's best and most original Santa, on Nov. 30th, 1989. He died while en route to entertaining children at Leighton School. We payed tribute to him a few days later, at the City Hall Christmas Lighting ceremony. Steve Pryor sent me this note about that evening. "The ceremony started around 6:30. By the time that you were to take the microphone it was just minutes before 7:00. One of the very first things you did was to talk about Bob McManus to the crowd. At the instant you mentioned Bob's name, church bells rang out to signify that it was 7:00. To borrow an analogy from "It's a Wonderful Life" as you did with Charlotte in your column, "an angel gets its wings every time a bell rings". It was a one in a million matter of timing that it played out that way. But for a kid who grew up and knew the real Santa Claus, it was clear that Bob did get his wings when you talked about him on Friday night December 1, 1989 at exactly 7:00 PM."

We planted a tree at City Hall in Bob's memory that year, as we noted his untimely passing. At that point, when those bells started to ring at St. Joseph's Church to mark the hour, and went on to play Silent Night, we saluted Santa for the last time.

The timing was perfect. The occasion was momentous. The loss of Oswego's most endeared and endearing Santa was all too real that Christmasy Night. No one has ever stepped in to fill his shoes, and probably no one ever will. He lives forever in our hearts, and in the warm and wonderful memories of countless Oswego children, now all grown, with children of their own, who will never forget the kind admonition of "Santa" Bob McManus, to "Love your brother and sisters, share your toys, and always respect your parents.... Oh, and keep a happy heart." Good advice from Oswego's Number One Santa of all time. His message is as important today as it was twenty years ago. The message to love one another at the holidays is one that will never grow old. Thank you Bob McManus for showing us the real spirit of Christmas.

And every time the bells ring out this season, take a moment to pause and remember Bob, think of how he got his wings, and say a little prayer for peace and goodwill, which he always spread in abundance.

John Sullivan, Jack Fitzgibbons, Gene Saloga

EUGENE G. SALOGA

Few people have had such a significant impact on the greater Oswego community as Gene Saloga, of East Sixth St. From his early days as a County Supervisor, to his later years as Oswego's Director of Community Development, with lots of other roles in between, Gene has been a pivotal force for much good in a community that he deeply loves and wants to see flourish.

I first met Gene when I was a freshman in college. He and Bob Chetney were great friends and political collaborators, and spent lots of time together plotting how to make Oswego County a better place. Bob and his wife Helen, and Gene and his wife to be, Julie Doyle, spent many an evening at Vona's restaurant, where people like Big Nick Sterio were fixtures at the bar, which was ably tended by Rocco Maniccia. On summer evenings, they would invariably wind up rounding out the night by sitting on the spacious screened in porch at the Chetney palazzo on W.. Seventh St., across from the hospital.

Several of my college friends lived there as boarders back then, and that's how I wound up on the front porch, sipping cocktails, and listening to Bob and Gene talk about County Government and local politics. I listened and learned a lot.

I even drove a sound truck acting as a get out the vote announcer for one of Bob Chetney's re-election campaigns. I confess, I supported Republicans back then. I even think I said "Vote Row A all the way" over the mike, through the tinny sounding loudspeakers affixed to the top of the Chetney station wagon by Art Vincent, a TV repairman and electronic gadget guru, who several years later I would run against for First Ward County Legislator.

My long relationship with Gene Saloga had begun, and it would end, career wise for Gene, when I was elected Mayor and brought him back from retirement to head the Community Development office. Gene Saloga is one of my proudest appointments. It was an honor for me to be able to bring him back into public service.

At that point, Gene had been President of the NYS Supervisors and County Legislator's Association, (now the NYS Association if Counties - NYSAC) Executive Assistant to Mayor Walter Lazarek, and Community Development Director under Mayor Jack FitzGibbons. He had also been a geologist and a Colonel in the U. S. Army reserves. He left government for a while to work for Niagara Mohawk as the head of the Nine Mile Point visitor's center. He had also married rather late in life, his long time girlfriend and my former next door neighbor, Julie Doyle, of West Seneca St. It was a marriage that would last a lifetime, until Julie's passing not long ago. My wife and I even named our second child Julie Ann (now Sierra) after Julie Doyle Saloga. Julie was a sweetheart, and the love of Gene's life.

One of my fondest memories of Gene and Julie is a visit they made to our tiny house on John St., after the birth of our daughter Julie, and just after I had graduated from law school. It was a long and celebratory evening, filled with laughter, camaraderie, and a pitcher or two of Martinis. I will never forget the look on Julie Saloga's face when, as Gene tried to make a point, he leaned and sunk the elbow of his sport coat deeply into the chip dip, seemingly unaware, and continuing his soliloquy as Julie and my wife Charlotte burst into fits of laughter over the sight of pipe smoking Gene, covered in cream cheese.

Gene was on the ground floor of much of the progress Oswego has made over the last forty years. The acquisition of the Naval Militia building, the siting of Indeck energy, the expansion of Alcan, the acquiring and developing of Wright's landing and its transformation from the "boathouses" to a marina, the concept and construction of the linear parks. They all bear Gene's signature conceptual design. Not to mention the Civic plaza, the renovation of the old post office, the sewage treatment plants, and the Water filtration facility. Suffice it to say that pretty much anything good that has happened in Oswego over the last four decades bears some mark of Gene's influence. His work product reflects a kind of quiet competence, as opposed to the bombasticity of some of his political mentors (myself included). But Gene's steady influence, and persistent efforts have truly born fruit, and for that, the community should be profoundly grateful. Gene Saloga is a one man vision squad who works well and plays well with others. His legacy is legendary, and his contributions enormous.

Thank you Gene, for being there for Oswego. Big time!

Anamae Mitchell and her husband Attorney Dick Mitchell

ANAMAE MITCHELL

When I was a teenage disc jockey for WOSC radio, I got to know the owner of the station, Anamae Mitchell, of E. River Road, Oswego, and back in those days, we, the radio station staff, billed ourselves as the "Fun Family", and so we gave her a nickname... "Mama Fun"! When I think of Anamae, I think of how fitting that nickname was. Anamae is a natural beauty, always perfectly coiffed and stylishly dressed, and always quick with a smile and a hearty laugh. She is just a delightful person to spend some time with, because whenever you're with Anamae, you know your going to have fun!

She is one of the famed Oswego beauties of the McGrath family, a daughter of William and Anna McMahin McGrath, and her sisters Helen (Benzing) who just passed away at the age of 94, Hazel (Ebert) of Californis, and Eileen (Ranous). Her brothers Jack and George McGrath died a few years ago. The McGrath girls could all have been contenders for the Miss America title in their heyday, and Anamae is the show stopper of the bunch. She and her late husband, renowned Oswego lawyer Richard C. Mitchell, were known to be great dancers who could show Fred Astaire and Ginger Rogers a step or two, and Anamae in her heyday was the Pearl Mesta of Oswego, who gave wonderful and joyous parties at the palatial Mitchell estate overlooking the east side of the Oswego River. On another note, I don't know what her brand of perfume is, but Anamae not only looks gorgeous, but she always smells great too!

She was the best radio ad salesperson ever. She would walk into McDonald's for Ladies Fashions, and Chauncey McDonald would just melt. It probably didn't hurt that she was one of his best customers too. She hired managers like Jack Burgess and Fred Maxin, but it was always clear who was the real boss. Anamae was in charge!

As a 16 year old disc Jockey at WOSC radio, I have many fond memories of my broadcasting days there on Lakeshore Rd. (It wasn't called Lakeshore road back then).

From 1962-64, every <u>Saturday morning,from 10-12</u>, I hosted a high school oriented rock and roll program entitled "The live 25 in Hi-Fi Jive". It featured call in requests, dedications, and the top 25 songs of the week, with call in quizzes and lots of lame humor!

Some of my early mentors, back in the day, were Frank Dale(real name Frank Michael Kaschak) the WOSC proverbial morning man, whose demeanor was gentle and friendly, but whose bad wig was always a source of amusement. You could always see where the roadkill type rug was glued onto his bald pate! A nicer guy though, you'd never find.

Another favorite of mine was Franny Mott, the afternoon Jazz loving DJ, who was wheelchair bound after a tragic car crash, and for whom the station was Made handicap accessible long before that was fashionable!

Wally Tucker was a Niagara college student who was a summer DJ, and later became station manager, and there was gruff Jack Burgess, the station manager, and voice of the Oswego Speedway, and Assistant Manager Fred Maxon, who would later become OHS Principal, and even later, Mayor of Fair Haven. And Helen Hennessey

Chetney, the Secretary, who herself later became a County Legislator, along with her Pall Times ad man husband Bob Chetney, of later real estate agency fame.

What a cast of characters they were! We billed ourselves as "the Fun Family" of Twin City Radio 1300, with studios in Fulton and Oswego. 1000 powerful watts of daytime AM radio! At the top of the organizational structure sat Anamae Mitchell.

There was the annual March of Dimes Tune Auction, the Polka music show with Frank on Sunday mornings, and the Italian American hour with Big Nick Sterio as host. Early Sunday afternoons. Anamae played a pivotal role in orchestrating all of this.

She always helped tonorganize the annual WOSC March of Dimes Tune Auction, with such CNY luminaries as Phil Markert as guest hosts. She made it possible for people like Frank Dale to host his Sunday Polish American hour, and for Nick Sterio to broadcast his weekly Italian American hour from the Oswego studios at the end of the bridge, in a building owned by her husband "Mitch", and her family still owns Old City Hall. And she supported a pimply faced teenager named Jack Sullivan in his quest to be a real life disc jockey., Anamae was a mentor to many, and a "Bon vivant" to all.

She also managed to raise three very independently minded children in the process, too. her daughter Marilyn became a teacher, while her son Richard became an attorney like his dad, and her daughter Pam, the Princess of the family, married Richard Palmer, who became an attorney and worked with her dad's law firm. They are all still fiercely devoted to their mother, who, rumor has it, has passed the century mark, and is still going strong! I am not sure if her family is planning a big shindig for her next milestone birthday, but I do know one thing, Now tat would be a birthday party worth attending! Here's wishing you many more years of health and happiness, Anamae!

John T. Sullivan Sr.

JOHN T. SULLIVAN SR.

Since Father's Day is soon approaching, I thought the best person to pay tribute to this month would be my dad, John T. Sullivan Sr. (1915-1983). Sully, as he was known to most of his friends, was a doer, a mover, and a shaker, who lit up any room he walked into by the sheer force of his very outgoing personality. He was a linotype operator "extraordinaire" by day, and a short order cook at night at Sully's diner, on West Bridge Sr., near the Forks of the road (where Friendly's Ice cream now stands.) He was a World War II veteran of the Amy Air Corps, as well.

My father always exhorted me to have "one job, and one job alone", as he felt he often stretched himself too thin with two and at times, even 3 jobs. I never did follow that advice. Maybe the apple didn't fall far after all. When I was running for Mayor, people criticized me for having too many things to do on my plate (lawyer, school attorney, Chair of the College Council, etc.) We answered that by saying, "Busy people get things done". While there is some truth to that, it is also true that burning the candle at several ends at once, can have a long term exhausting effect.

For several years he would work <u>7am-3 pm</u> at the Pall Times, setting type, then deliver papers on a rural route that went as far as Pulaski, then come home for a quick supper with family before heading to his diner to work the night shift scrambling eggs, flipping pancakes, and serving up Sully's famous original Texas Hots. It was Sully's Texas Hot recipe that Rudy Gadzalia envied, but my dad would never sell it to him, despite Rudy's repeated entreaties. There was an interesting story about how he originally got the recipe, and it involved an all night card game at a place in Rochester called "Machine Gun Charlie's", but that's the stuff for another column someday.

My dad closed the diner in 1956, and after that, Rudy finally made his own wannabe sauce based on Sully's, but it was just that, a second class replica of the real thing (with all due apologies to Carol Livesey and her son Jason). Sully's Texas hots were and are still the best, with their special ingredients (which included cinnamon and paprika, but no tomato sauce). You had to "cook it down", my dad would say, when making a batch of it. The sweet smell of the real deal Texas hot sauce is a scent that lingers with you for a lifetime!

Sully was always involved in something. He became President of the local typesetter's union, which was part of the ITU (International Typographical Union). He was involved in the local Moose Club, and became Governor of the Moose Lodge 743, a job which he proudly held for several years. As kids, we always enjoyed the annual Moose Lodge Christmas party, and stories about Moose Haven, and other great eleemosynary activities of the Benevolent order. He was also named Chief Agimitator of the Moose Club, and given a trophy for that dubious honor, which I still have and proudly display. An "Agimitator", it seems, is someone who walks into a room, riles everyone up, gets them jousting with one another, and then slips out the door with a smile on his face. His fraternal activities didn't stop there. He was a member of the Elks, the American Legion, the VFW, and the Ancient Order of Hibernians, where he would tend bar in his retirement years.

Dad also held the city concession license to sell soda pop and hot dogs at Otis field during the high school football games, and at the

Oswego Genesee Baseball games. He also had a stand at the Fort Ontario Softball fields, where he sold his wares. He and his partner in culinary crime, Dave Henderson, were as famous for their popcorn stands, as for their Texas Hots. I remember one Saturday when dad came home after a long day of concessioneering, and we were all running down the street to a neighbor's house to watch the Mickey Mouse club on our neighbor's new TV. Not to be outdone, dad went across the street from our house to Gover's Department Store, and plunked down $500 cash (the days earnings, from Otis Field, which had to be an enormous sum back then) for a new TV on condition that they would deliver it immediately. He wanted his kids to be with him, not off watching someone else's tv. I will never forget in later years when we kids got together and bought my parents a new color tv, and dad came home from a long day at work, and then, no doubt, Wood's bar and Grill, only to fall asleep on the couch and to awaken watching Huntley/Brinkley, while we waited for his reaction. It took a while, but he finally exclaimed.. "Color..It's in color!", as he choked up like the sentimental Irishman he always was. That is one of my fondest memories. We pulled a fast one on Sully!

Sully's impact on the community was substantial, as was the legacy he left us, and the impact his children would have on Oswego as well. I know he was as proud of us as he was his "Bloody 5th Ward" Irish Heritage. It is comforting for us to know that his Irish eyes are forever smiling down on us from above. Happy Father's Day, John Thomas Sullivan Sr. Your spirit endures, and is as "Welcome as the flowers in May!" We miss you, Dad!

DEMOCRAT candidate for Mayor, Jack Fitzgibbons, and his family, all members of whom are participating in his door-to-door campaign, are shown above. Left to right are Jerome, Ellen, Mary, Jeanne, his wife Joan, John Jr., the candidate himself, Joanie and Kathleen.

Whole Fitzgibbons Family Campaigns

Fitzgibbons Family

JACK FITZGIBBONS

When a Pope or an Arcbishop dies, it is often written of them that they were "Beloved" by their people. To be beloved, is to be regarded with much affection. And respect. Or, as the poet Maya Angelou put it, "You may not always remember what a person says to you, or what a person does to you, but you will always remember how they made you feel".

If one word can capture the essence of a person's character, "beloved" works when it comes to describing John Edward Timothius FitzGibbons of East Seventh St. in Oswego.

"Jack" FitzGibbons, as he is known to friends and family, is a man who gives much love to his family and his community, and as a result, is much loved in return. He and his late wife Joan Galvin Fitzgibbons raised seven amazing children in their spacious and joyous home on East Seventh St. They did so with much mirth and merriment, and lots and lots of love. And at the ripe young age of 89 on his next birthday this May 6th, Jack indeed lives, loves, thrives and continues to be cherished by his family, his friends, and the community. It just doesn't get much better than the life lived by Jack Fitzgibbons.

I have often said that if I knew that I had but an hour to live, and could choose one person to have a last conversation with before being called by my maker, that person would be Jack Fitzgibbons!

Our acquaintance dates back to 1975, the year I graduated law school, and returned to Oswego to practice law under the tutelage of John O'Connor Conway. His brother-in-law, Jack Fitzgibbons, was asked by John to run for Mayor that year, as the Democratic nominee in a campaign against the incumbent, and well regarded Walter Lazarek. John asked me to be Jack Fitzgibbons' campaign manager, and as they say, the rest is, well, local history.

And a grand history it is! We won that mayoral campaign by a mere 117 votes. We beat a popular incumbent, and that was no small accomplishment. I remember riding herd on Jack to go and knock on at least ten doors a night. I remember the photo of all seven of the Fitzy kids, some of whom were perched on and under, and even hanging from the limbs of a neighborhood tree. It was a great photo! (see photo attached)

We even had a cool bumper sticker, "Back Jack Fitz", and a nifty campaign song, sung to the tune of "Let me call you sweetheart"..... "Vote for Jack Fitzgibbons, he's the one for you. He will be our Mayor for the best of old and new. If you love Oswego, and you care about your town...Vote for Jack Fitzgibbons, he's the best there is around"!

Jack became Mayor for two, 2 year terms. He presided over our celebration of the national bi-centennial, acquired the former Naval militia building on Lake St. (now known as the McCrobie building) for municipal purposes from the state, and began the process of building the west side marina with the replacement of the "boathouses below the bank near Wright's Landing. Jack named Rosemary Nesbitt as City historian, and started her on the road to civic involvement which resulted in the H. Lee White maritime museum, among other accomplishments.

He created a bi partisan City Chsrter Commission (naming yours truly as Chairman) which rewrote the City Charter, strengthened the role of Mayor, made it a four year term, and created the City Personnel department replacing the Civil Service Commission. The crowning achievement of Jack's four years as Mayor was the salvage of and reconstruction of Oswego City Hall, and it's adaptation as a modern municipal facility.

Jack actually offered me the job of Executive Assistant, which I was grateful for, but turned down when I learned that I had passed the bar exam. I am pleased to say that I played a role in grooming and selecting Art O'Neill as his Executive Assistant. Art turned out to be an excellent choice, I was also happily involved in the decision to retain Walt Lazarek's Executive Assistant, Gene Saloga, a Republican, and to name him as Community Development Director. That proved to be another of Jack's great choices.

In later years, when Jack became the Executive Director of the Port Authority, and I became Mayor, we didn't always see eye to eye on how to develop the Port. It didn't affect our long friendship however, which endured, despite our differences. Jack is one of those rare individuals in political life with whom you could disagree, but never be disagreeable with. He taught me much. He added new words to my lexicon like Opie dildoc, and "Let's have a smile!" I listened and learned what his late father George would say about burning bridges behind you, which you should never do, because you never know in life when you might have to retreat over that same bridge. That advice has proved invaluable to me, through the years.

He also made me understand how family values really means valuing your family. He has that special Irish lilt in his voice, in his step, and in his demeanor, and when he sings "Believe me if all these endearing young charms, or recites a Thomas Moore poem, you just know that Jack Fitzgibbons is the real deal. He is a community treasure. He is much beloved by his friends, family, and the entire Oswego community.

As the words of that old song go, the greatest gift, is to love, and be loved in return."

Jack Fitzgibbons has an abundance of love in his life. Oswego is fortunate to have him and his family's continued presence in abundance. So Happy 89th birthday Jack! And many many more!

Joan and Will Schum

WILL SCHUM

I think there is an old adage that kind of sums up the life of Will Schum---"Where there's a will, there's a way". Truer words were never spoken—Without Will…this event would not be taking place.

Let me briefly tell you the story of how the Safe Haven museum project came about. In 1988, I learned about a PBS documentary about Ruth Gruber's book, Safe Haven. I had lived in Oswego all of my life, yet I did not know the story, and at the age of 41. I had just been elected Mayor of Oswego. So, I said to my Executive Assistant, Eli Rapaport.. We've got to do something abut this, so we formed the Safe Haven Committee to expore the idea of creating a museum on the site to commemorate that capter in Oswego and America's history. I actually campaigned, unsuccessfully, for Oswego to be chosen as the site for the National Holocaust museum. We lost out to the nation's capital on that one, but not to be deterred, I appointed the newly retired Principal of the Campus School, Will Schum, to head up the Safe Haven committee..and as they say..the rest is history.

Will spearheaded the formation of a 501C 3 NFP corporation, and began to raide funds, and we got a number of Jewish Community Activists from the CNY community involved to help support the effort, and after 16 long years..the museum finallycame to be..it was a long hard slog, but with Will's help, and Judy and Eli and dozens of others, it finally became a reality.

Every time I come home to Oswego, I drive up onto the Harbor lookout over Wright's Landing,just to gaze at the Oswego Light House. To me, it is a beacon of hope that shines brightly on the Harbor, and has guided many a weary seafarer into the Safe Haven of the Harbor. In many ways, Oswego itself, and the fort Ontario refugee center stood as the only beacon of hope during WWI, when 982 refugees were rescued from the ravages of war town Europe, and made their way here to Oswego for the duration of the war, and eventually freedom. Amd as they arose every morning on the windswept shores of Lake Ontario and the Harbor, that lighthouse stood as a symbol of hope for a brighter future for all of them.

If any one individual could be said to define, by his very persona, the concept of community service, that one person would be Dr. Willard C. Shum. Will Schum was born in the Buffalo suburb of Cheektowaga, and attended Buffalo State University, where he ultimately obtained a Doctoral degree in Education. A Navy veteran of the Korean War, Will married his college sweetheart, Joan Kilma, and moved to Oswego NY to become the Principal of the then Campus School (Swetman Learning Center). He later retired as an Associate Dean, from State University College at Oswego.

Will was always a very active member of the Rotary club, and continued to be until the time of his demise in September 2013. Through Rotary, Will also became involved in the Partnership for the Americas project, and was instrumental in establishing a relationship between his hometown of Oswego, N.Y. and the tiny Republic of Montserrat, which later was devastated by a massive volcanic eruption in 1997. He spearheaded efforts to provide relief to the volcano victims of that tragedy, and was also active in the American Field Service program for hosting Foreign exchange students for many years.

After his retirement, Will was recruited by me as Mayor to assist in a project of establishing a museum to commemorate the role of Oswego and Fort Ontario in the rescue and housing of 982 refugees from Nazi Germany during World War II. This little known chapter in history is much better known, now that Will has been involved. Indeed, he spearheaded the formation of the museum committee, and today, the Safe Haven Fort Ontario Museum is not only a reality, but planning a major expansion. Will's leadership was essential in the drive to bring about the Safe Haven museum, and his commitment and dedication to the project from the start was unwavering, without Will, this just would not have happened.

Will met his wife Joan at a coffee shop while in college, and two sons and 55 years of marriage later, they were inseparable until his death last fall. Will had heart problems for several years before he died, but it did not deter him from his rounds as a volunteer at the hospital in Venice, Fla, where he and Joan maintained a winter retirement home. He was also active in Rotary up until the day he died.

"Will just loved people", said his wife Joan. "He just would not stop doing things for people, no matter how badly he felt. He was like the Ever ready energizer bunny when it came to helping those in need. He just cared. He cared a lot", she added. Schum's association with Safe Haven dated from 1988, when he was named to chair a committee to investigate the establishment of a museum, and continued with his involvement on the board until just recently. He particularly enjoyed talking with some of the refugees, and hearing of their experiences first hand. The establishment of the Safe Haven museum was his greatest non-academic achievement. He had many other pluses in his long career in education, and his wife Joan is still answering notes and letters from his former colleagues and students who have written to tell of how Will affected their lives in a positive way.

Will's life stands as a beacon for his students, his friends and family, and his Rotary community, and surely for his friends at the Safe Haven museum. Thank you Will! Your life and your work made all the difference!

David and Mary Roman and daughter Elizabeth

DAVID JOHN ROMAN

I first met David John Roman in the fall of 1976. He was being interviewed by John Conway as a possible part time law clerk. He was also being considered for a part time job with our law office, consisting of both Mike Shanley and myself. At the time, we were located in the Mil-Mar building, on the second floor, at the corner of West First and Bridge Streets It is the building that later housed King Arthur's restaurant.

David was an alumnus of the Cornell School of Labor relations and Albany Law School, and his dad, John Roman, was a top executive with Utica Blue Cross/Blue Shield, and he was from Rome, N.Y. His mother Betty was a legal secretary, and they raised 7 children on their Oriskany farm. His dad knew Judge Conway, which is how Dave got the interview. He landed the job on his own merits, however, for certain.

Once you met David, it didn't take long to form the impression that he was very bright, very hard working, and very conscientious. All traits which have served him well over the years. When all else fails, you can always rely on David to be there. He is more dependable than Big Ben the clock, and like Miniver Cheevy, you can set your watch by him.. Once he starts something, he stays on the task until completed, and he will leave no stone unturned in so doing.

He also has an amazing memory, which I think is akin to genius level. If you don't believe me, just ask him how much it would cost in playing Monopoly if you landed on Marvin Gardens with three houses on it. Dave can tell you. He memorized the monopoly board. His ability to digest and recall huge quantities of information in a hard drive on fast forward kind of way, served him very well when he served for twenty years as Oswego County's Family Court Judge. He could have a stack of twenty files on his desk, and he could tell you the essential details on each file he reviewed, in amazing detail. He never forgets a thing. That is mostly good. But if you get on the wrong side of him, it can work against you big time. Just ask some of the repeat litigants who appeared before him and thought that they could pull the wool over his eyes and bamboozle him as a Judge. That just didn't happen. Judge Roman didn't forget.

Dave became the Family Court Judge in a kind of unusual way, and it involved a cross endorsement by both political parties to allow him to do so, and to succeed long time Family Court Judge Donald K. Comstock, who retired in 1986. Dave had been Judge Comstock's law clerk after serving as Judge Conway's clerk. He served ten years after being elected as a Democrat, and was then forced to change his party enrollment to seek re-election for a second ten year term, given Oswego County's strong proclivity for electing Republicans. He really had no choice in the matter, but I think it always bothered him a bit. Politics was never Dave's forte. His real talents lay in fair, compassionate and timely justice from the bench. In fact, he did not like politics at all, and so when he had to run in a Republican primary to keep the job he had done so well, for over twenty years, politics triumphed, and we lost a very talented Family Court Judge at the top of his game. Fortunately, His career didn't end there. He was named a Judicial Hearing officer by the Office of Court Administration, a job he held for several years.

He did hearings three days a week in Family Court in Syracuse, and then, more recently, was named as a part time City of Oswego Judge by Mayor Tom Gillen. He still serves in that capacity several days a week. Ironically, he is an assistant Judge to our former intern and one time law partner, Jamie Metcalf, who once served as Dave's Family Court law clerk.. There is more than a little irony here. I kid him about that almost every time I see him. The point is, he is still serving the people of this state as a Judge, which he does so well, and loves to do. That's a very good thing.

He also loves to play golf, which he didn't always like to do, or do so well, but he has gotten better at it over the years. Persistence pays.

Dave is decidedly parsimonious. He is more a saver than a spender, and while I won't claim that he still has his first communion money, he does have lots of $100 dollar savings bonds that he faithfully bought every bi weekly paycheck for the past forty plus years. He has also made some wise and bountiful investments, much against my terrible financial advice. I remember him asking me many years ago about whether he should invest in buying part of a gas station, and I told him he'd be crazy to do so. Thirty years, three gas stations, and very substantial increases in the value of his investments later, it is me who is eating crow, while David could feast on caviar, if he chose to, which he never will.

I am the kind of guy who sold Apple stock at $35 dollars, thinking it could never go any higher. Not so, David Roman. He has done very well, investing smartly over the years. Someone told him in college that he should have been an actuarial underwriter. He did not choose that path, thankfully, much to the benefit of many thousands of Oswego County citizens and their families.

Dave has served for so long on so many community boards and volunteer positions, I have lost count. He has been a Y board member forever. We used to play racquetball there 3 times a week for twenty years. He serves his college fraternity and has for 30 plus years, and is now the Grand pooh-bah of Sigma Phi Epsilon on a national level. He still serves on a Statewide Judicial ethics panel, and at one point, was even the head of the Family Court Judges organization for NYS.

David Roman is a dependable friend, neighbor, and recently even an almost full time care giver for our friend Tish Kelly, who grew ill, and in need of lots of help, before she recently died. You could always depend on "Good old Dave" to be there. He is probably the most loyal, consistent and caring friend anyone could ever ask for.

He is also a devoted father to his bright and talented daughter Elizabeth, and an ever faithful and supportive husband to his lovely wife Mary. He is the relied upon brother by his 6 siblings, and everyone in the Roman family's favorite uncle. All in all, David Roman is not just a pretty good guy. He is, most of all, my lifelong adulthood good and loyal friend, and you can take that to the bank. They just don't come along very often like David John Roman.

Kathy and Ed Matott

ED AND KATHY MATOTT

What happens when the Kappa Sigma Teen Queen of the year marries the future Principal of the Oswego Middle School? Magic, that's what, and a fairytale life! I am talking about my lifelong friends Eddie Matott and Kathy Fleischman Matott, who have now been married, and happily so, for over 47 years.

Eddie and Kathy were the second best jitterbugging couple of the OCHS class of 1964, second only of course to Charlotte and myself. Ed will try to tell you that he is in first place, but I have the trophy from a 1962 dance contest to prove it. They didn't call me "Boppin John L" for nothing. I would give them first place, however, for their dancing routine to Dion and the Belmont's "Runaround Sue". That one they just nail.

My acquaintance with Ed Matott dates back to Kindergarten. I think he sat at the blue table. I sat at the red table. We joined the Cub Scouts together. His mother was our Cub Scout den mother. We played on the Kindergarten basketball team together. Then, he moved from the corner of Ontario and Van Buren Sts. to Hamilton Homes, on the east side, and became a St. Paul's kid. He was a transplanted west sider, forced to live in an east side world. I always thought that Ed's redeeming qualities lay in his St. Mary's roots.

His redeeming judgment was in having the eminent good sense to court and pursue a relationship with Kathy Fleischman, an East Fifth St. beauty with solid credentials and deep Oswego Irish bona fides.

Kathy was elected one of our high school fraternity's "Teen Queens" of the month, and was voted Teen Queen of the year in 1962. She deserved the title. She still does. A graduate of CCBI in Syracuse, while Ed graduated from Oswego State, they married in 1967, and have lived happily ever after since. Ed became a middle school science teacher, then a Vice Principal under the venerable Carl Palmitesso, and then Principal himself. He also ran for 6th Ward Alderman in Oswego, and was elected to five terms. He used up a lot of shoe leather in his five campaigns, but he got to know the wants and needs of his constituents, and he represented them ably on the Common Council. He was a great public servant. He has resisted efforts to draft him to run for Mayor. I for one wish he would stop resisting and just do it. Oswego would be the better for it. He still volunteers for city beautification projects, and keeps tabs on how the city looks when he and Kathy take their many walks through their beloved hometown.

In the last several years, Florida has beckoned, and Ed and Kathy have answered by staying several months in the sunshine state as snow birds in Sarasota. More power to them.

As a science teacher, Ed was a standout. As Principal, he was tough, but fair, and the kids respected "Mr. Matott"! His detractors would say that he brought an "attitude" to the job, while his supporters would say he brought his heart and soul. Such is the job of a Principal, you are never entirely right. You must contend with the cross constituencies of parents, kids, teachers, and School Board members, and to navigate those sometimes choppy waters successfully is no small achievement, and navigate the waters he did.

Ed is a person who cares about his friends. He cares about his community, and he cares about his wife and family, as rightfully he should. Kathy is on the successful back end of a bout with breast cancer, and is today vibrant and healthy, much to both Kathy and Ed's credit. They never gave up and they stayed positive, walked it off together, and it worked out for the best. Ed had a bout with cancer as well, and beat it back. He is a fighter. Some even have described him as a "banty rooster" type. My father always kidded him about his resemblance to Andy Griffith's side kick Don Knotts, as "Barney Fife". He is a little wiry and quick to opine about everything, but that's the beauty of Eddie Matott.

Ed and Kathy are the proud parents of three children, Mary Kathleen, Matthew, and Michael, and the grandparents of five, Daniel, Jack, Maggie, Mark and Christopher.

"Mr. Matott" always kids me on Facebook about my "hands on hip poses", but he is the first one to pose in similar fashion, or to fold his arms when lecturing you. But he always means well, and what he has to say is important. I have grown to appreciate his friendship and counsel. He has always been there, in good times and in bad, and his constant rock solid friendship is something I have come to value and indeed, cherish. The Principal and the beauty queen turned out to be a fantastic match, and almost everything they needed to know, they learned in Kindergarten. We are just lucky that they continue to share their wisdom and love for each other and for the Oswego community with all who enjoy their much valued presence.

Barb and Sam Domicolo

Sam Domicolo

SAM DOMICOLO

"Lake Ontario...Harborfest Oswego! People come on, come out, people come on now jump and shout!"

That's the opening line from my favorite Harborfest theme song, and it was the winning entry for the year 1990, and was written and ably performed by Oswego native Sam Domicolo. "Sam" as he is now professionally known in Venice, Florida, where he and his wife Barbara Perry, former Minetto elementary school principal, live during the fall and winter months.

Sam has a big and loyal, almost groupie like following in his adopted second home in Florida. And why not? He sounds better now than he did when he was 17 and singing in the "Kings Three" with Mike Pauldine and Gary Stevens. They were the stars who performed at my late wife Charlotte's "Sweet 16" party in Hopkins Hall, beneath St. Mary's church. They were a Kingston Trio wannabe group, and they were good. Very good. Tom Dooley's head never hung down better than with Sam at the microphone.They performed in the DG premier on the Oswego Theatre stage, and in many other venues. And they morphed into several other groups in the coming years.

My favorite high school group featuring Sam was "The Valiants", with Danny Kraft, Jimmy Losurdo, Buzz McFarland, and Dickie Hillman. Those guys really rocked the house. The usual venue was Christ Church Hall, where Sam reminds me that I used to bring two shirts to the dances, since I always sweated entirely through the first one, and needed a wardrobe change. Those Valiants really put us through our dance paces. and if you don't believe me, just ask Eddie Matott.

After High school, Sam joined the Navy, and served on board the USS Truckee, a navy oil ship, during the Vietnam conflict. He came home and worked in several jobs, but music was always his first love. He never gave up his day jobs as a pharmacist assistant, salesman at times, and finally, as a school janitor, but it was always the music that continued to float Sam's boat. It was his first love, in addition to his sons Michael, Anthony and Ryan, in whom he takes great pride, and his four grandchildren, Kali, Joey, Danielle and Jordan. But Barb is the wind beneath his wings, and has enabled him to exclusively pursue music as a first career, and it works.

There were many other groups Sam performed with over the years. Some names come to mind... "The Newberry Four", "The Dude Potatoes', the "Watermelons", "The Critics", and one of my favorites, the "Edge of Darkness" which featured a black hearse as their band wagon and musicians Vic DiDominick, Paul Fergusen, and Chip Riley. Sam is finally a solo act, billed as just "Sam". Eat your heart out Prince or Madonna, we have Sam!

On a recent trip to Florida, I drove a couple of hundred miles out of my way just to surprise him and to hear him sing at the Cafe Venice, where he holds forth on Thursday nights. He is a legend there and here, and has earned the right to be called legendary "Sam". As a solo act, he excels, and when he sings "A taste of your wine..red red wine..." the audience sings along as enthusiastically as they do when he belts out the Neil Diamond classic "Sweet Caroline". It is happy, sing along, have a glass of wine and enjoy type music, and we baby boomers can't get enough of it. Sam and Barb spend their summers in Oswego, where he performs at several local venues on a regular basis, including Alex's on the Water, Old City Hall, and Gibby's.

Today, Sam is on top of his game. He has had his ups and downs in life, as have we all. In his profession, what career musician hasn't? A recent low point came with the death of his lifelong best friend Joe Spereno, the best sax player I have ever heard. Joe and Sam date back to 1949, when Sam, as a four year old immigrant from Italy, learned to speak English with the assistance of his friend and neighbor, Joe. He misses Joe very much. We all do.

Sam was the oldest of five children born to Italian immigrants Michael and Sally Domicolo, and was followed by siblings Carm, Michael, Dave (who is a performer in his own right) and Maria. He is justifiably proud of his Italian roots, and has traveled back to visit the homeland on several occasions.

Most importantly though, Sam has stayed true to his passion, made merry with his music, and charmed, entertained, and enhanced the lives of hundreds of his fans by just singing his songs, and singing them so well. Wherever Sam sings people come out, and still jump and shout. And that's a good thing. A very good thing!

Nancy and Joe Rodak

NANCY RODAK

There are some people who are just ...larger than life. Nancy Joyce Rodak was one of those individuals. Nance never just walked into a room, she made an entrance. Her very presence was a statement. Nancy not only had an outsized personality, but she was also a woman with a plus size figure who dressed well for all occasions, smelled great, and just exuded feminine charm. She always carried herself with a certain kind of savoir faire, a panache, that left an impression on anyone who had the pleasure to make her acquaintance.

She grew up in the "Flats" area of the First Ward in Oswego, where her family ran a bakery. The Flats were the area below 5th St., and North of Seneca St. to the Harbor. It was an area that had a "Coal Shaker" on the Coal Trestle and a Great Lakes ship called the "Fontana" that docked there often, bringing midwest coal for the Steam Plant to burn. Nancy's combination of French and Irish heritage made for a unique mix of fun loving, laughter, and shrewd sophistication. Some say that when she married Joe Rodak, with his Polish practicality, they had it all.

Joe was a 7th Ward Oswegonian, who attended the University of Vermont and became an engineer. Joe and Nancy moved to Florida and then Texas, where they had two children, Joey and Lisa, who grew up to be talented and successful individuals in their own right, Joe as a lawyer and Lisa as a Tourism professional.

The Rodaks moved back to Oswego in the mid 70's, where Joe took a job with his brother-in-law Billy Joyce, as a manager in his trucking and warehousing company, Oswego Stevedoring. The couple bought a large home at the corner of West Third and Mohawk Sts. in Oswego. Nancy entered into a hair salon business with her cousin, Alma Joyce Holland, who was also a pronounced presence in her own special way. She renamed herself Alexandra. The two Joyce girls collaborated in the salon Business on West Bridge St. Just west of Liberty, near the Forks of the road. It was called "The House of Joyce". They employed several talented hairstylists including Ian Wills and Roger Dolan, and it proved to be a very popular hairdressing and styling venue.

In later years, Joe and Nancy opened a bar and restaurant on Rt. 104 near Sheldon Avenue, and called it, "The Caberet"., and what a Caberet it was. They had live entertainment on weekends and often a New Orleans ragtime group on Sunday's to the delight of their many patrons.

They also were the local franchisee for "Sal's Birdland" chicken wings and BBQ sauce, and did a land office take out business.

I remember Joe asking my advice as to whether I thought a chicken wing franchise would go in Oswego. His son Joey, who attended St. John Fisher College in Rochester, raved about the sauce formula. I told Joe I didn't think anyone would buy just chicken wings. Years earlier, I had eaten a "whammy dinner" of 21 chicken wings from the Parkside Drive In on the way back to the college from a long day at Buckland's, and I got terribly sick. So I was a no go on chicken wings for a long time. Boy was I wrong. The Sal's Birdland BBQ wings were a huge success. Almost as great a success as the Caberet itself.

Nancy held court there most nights, especially on the weekends, from a corner chair at the end of the bar where she would sit with her turbaned hairdo and a long cigarette holder, and dispense savvy advice to her many patrons.

Her favorite song was Satin Doll. That may be where the "cigarette holder" came in. She would occasionally get up and sing that song after constant prodding by her customers, and she always brought down the house. I used to kid her and call her "Nancy with the laughing eyes", from another old song.

When I decided to step down as County Democratic Chair in 1979, I chose Joe Rodak to succeed me. Joe did a great job. He later served in my Mayoral administration in several capacities. He was a pretty savvy guy, but somehow, Joe could never quite get out from under Nancy's shadow. Oswego City Historian Rosemary Nesbitt would often introduce Joe at political gatherings as "Mr. Nancy Rodak". Joe and Nancy became good friends with Charlotte and me, and many a laugh was shared. I also valued Nancy's often sage advice. Somehow, she just knew if things were right or not, and cautioned accordingly. When I was first thinking about running for Mayor, one of the first person's counsel and advice I sought was Nancy's. She wasn't wildly enthusiastic about the idea, but she knew of my love for politics, and she encouraged me to follow my dreams.

Nancy was forever giving advice, and pulling things out of her purse and giving them to people. Sometimes it was a handkerchief to absorb a tear, other times it was a rosary, or a holy card, or a recipe, or any number of things that just seemed to fit the particular occasion. Her purse was like a magic bag of tricks, and when it came to problems, she had a fix for everything, and if you had a chance to talk with Nancy, somehow you wound up knowing that happiness was just around the bend, prosperity just around the corner, and if you just hung in there, things would be all right.

Just one look at her big, haunting, and beautiful eyes, and that knowing twinkle, and you could be laughing out loud one minute, and crying the next. For Nancy, life was indeed a "Caberet". Her motto always seemed to be, just like the song, "What good is sitting alone in your room? Come, hear the music play. Life is a caberet old chum, so come to the Caberet.Come hear the band, come taste the wine, come blow your horn, start celebrating, right this way your table's waiting...". I can think of no better song to express Nancy's zest for life, which all us who came to know her felt. Not bad advice at all.

Dory and Ed Lisk

ED LISK

Much of life is about leaving a legacy, and to leave a legacy, you must engage in lifelong learning, all the while, loving what you do. If there be a model for success in that department, one very distinguished Oswego native stands out as "First in class ". His name is Edward S. Lisk. I am proud to know him, and to call him a friend.

Indeed we've got talent, right here in River City! It begins with E and it ends with K, and it's spelled ED LISK. River City had its mythical music man in the person of Professor Harold Hill, and Oswego has its very own, very real, and very accomplished "Music Man" in Ed Lisk! He not only knows how to play and conduct, but he has been a mentor to many, a musician's musician, and is truly entitled to be called the "Leader of the band!"

Ed grew up in Oswego in a home where only Polish was spoken. English was his second language, and he learned to play clarinet as a way of being able to express himself, musically, in ways he could not yet do verbally. That would later change dramatically, as he learned to not only express himself musically, but verbally, and with the written word as well, to the point where his written works have become the bible for thousands of band teachers and music educators across the United States,. They read his methods books and articles, and adapt his type of teaching into their own programs. His is a record of remarkable success, emulated widely by other musicians/educators and conductors in dozens of states..

Ed was educated in local schools, and at SUNY Oswego and Syracuse University, and returned to his native Oswego in 1970, when he accepted the position of Director of Music, while being charged by the Oswego School Superintendent at the time, to develop an outstanding music program, and that he assuredly did, over the next 21 years. His Wind ensembles became legendary, and the Oswego School music program K-12 became the envy of school districts across the state for its many successes. He recruited exceptional talent to the program. Ed put his hometown "Marching Buccaneers" on the national map quickly. They marched in big time national parades, and won all kinds of awards and accolades in statewide and national competitions. He brought the pride back into the Oswego Schools music program, With the likes of Bill Palange, Tony Joseph, Bill Crist and others who continued the tradition, Ed Lisk singlehandedly resurrected a somewhat moribund music program at Oswego, made it second to none, and the envy of all. He did Oswego proud.

I was Mayor of Oswego when Ed retired in 1991. I was proud to have presented him with the Key to the City upon his retirement, and he often reminds me of the letter I wrote to him, which he still has framed above his desk at home. Here is what I wrote to him in 1991 :

"It has been said that music comes from the soul and that the heart is the key to the soul. There is certainly no question but that you have been both the heart and the soul of the Oswego School District music program for many years, ever since your decision to return to your hometown. You have raised our sights and our spirits; you have given of yourself until it sometimes hurt; and all the while, we, the citizens of Oswego, have been the recipients of the many benefits of your stewardship....."

Oswego's loss was the country's gain, as Ed began to travel widely and become a Nationally recognized conductor and music educator. He was chosen as the President of the National Band Masters Association, and has taught, guest conducted, and mentored music programs in almost all of the 50 states, earning high praise and recognition from his musical colleagues along the way. One such Music educator put it this way, "At a time of dramatic educational and societal change, when thinking and values of the past have been cast aside, Ed Lisk has established himself as a unique leader in the profession. His ideas and methods are utilized daily by hundreds of band directors throughout the nation. And it is making a difference - Ed's contribution to the profession is beyond measure and his integrity as an educator is beyond reproach. "Bobby Adams, Ph.D., Director of Bands, Stetson University. John Phillips Sousa could not have said it better.

Who would have thought that after 21 years at Oswego he would go on for another 22 years, traveling, conducting and continuing to teach, write and mentor? Most importantly, he shows no signs of letting up yet.

Ed and his beautiful wife Dorie, continue to make Oswego their home, as they travel widely. I always enjoy seeing them at their favorite (and mine too) Oswego restaurant, Canale's, when I am home! We share a laugh and reminisce, and speak of things yet to come. I know he's as proud of his daughters Carol Ann and Jean, their husbands, Bill Crist, and David Buske, and his six grandchildren, and even three great grandchildren, as he is of his professional accomplishments.

To quote from the Band Master himself:

"My goal for the Oswego School District was to bring national recognition for its academic excellence. This was not difficult for me as my personal expectations were high and I never doubted that I could achieve this goal. As I travel, lecture, and guest conduct, I emphasize to teachers and students to live a life of truth and dignity. Strive for excellence in everything you do and never be satisfied with less than your best. We are only here on this earth to give and share with others."

Well said, Mr. Lisk, and I might add, well done too!

F. Hosmer Culkin

F. HOSMER CULKIN

I quit smoking almost thirty years ago. I smoked from the age of seventeen to 37, and when I turned 37, I remembered a casual comment made by Hosmer Culkin, a respected blue blood attorney and head of the Culkin clan. He told me, if you don't smoke more than 20 years, your lungs will make a comeback, and you"ll have no long term effects. Why did he say that, and why did I take it to heart? I don't know. He was not a doctor, he was just Hosmer, but I guess when he spoke, I regarded him as a professional icon, and I took whatever he said to heart. ANd best of all, it made me quit, cold turkey, on turning 37. I just thought of what Hosmer said, and I never touched another cigarette again.

When he was in his 90"s and starting to show his age, I reminded him of that when I bumped into him at Canale's one night. He had no recollection of it at all. It made me think of how, from time to time, people will say to me, "I remember what you said about such and such, and that was good advice you gave me." Often, I haven't a clue as to what I said. (I just like to spout)..but whatever Hosmer said and did had a profound impact on his family, friends, and in a larger sense, the entire Oswego Community. I always enjoyed Hosmer's company, and the many stories he would tell. More on that in a minute.

Hosmer was very active in politics, although he never ran for office. I think he may have crossed party lines to vote for me for Mayor, but I can't be sure about that. He was a pretty solid Republican in the best sense of what the Republican party used to stand for. Today, they would probably call him a RINO (Republican in name only), and I know that many of his children have not always continued to tow the party line. I think part of the reason I liked Hosmer was that he was just smart, and very witty, and principled as well. He could dish it out pretty good, but he wasn't as good at taking it. Maybe that's why he never actually threw his hat in the ring to run for office himself. His father was a venerable Congressman, and maybe one Congressman Culkin per family is enough.

I grew up knowing the Culkin kids. There were 7 children, one child dying shortly after childbirth. Betsy was a classmate of mine, and Florence was in my sister's class. Frank was a bit older, and the late Mary Louise older too. I did not know the younger kids, Billy, and Josephine, but suffice it to say the Culkins are a great, and lively bunch, and have dispersed all across the country, several of them, including Frank, to Colorado, where Hosmer and his wonderful wife, the late Florence Kiley Culkin, often travelled to visit.

One of my funniest Hosmer Cullkin stories involves my first year as a lawyer. Hosmer had visited our offices in the Mil-Mar building (later King Arthur's steakhouse) for a real estate closing, and I had been in a deposition all morning. It was a rainy day, and when I emerged to go to lunch, I found that Hosmer had mistakenly taken my rubber galoshes, instead of his, and his were too small to fit me. So, I called his secretary Carol, and asked for Hosmer, and he wasn't there, so I said to Carol, who was always very prim and proper like an old school librarian, "Carol, do you know if Hosmer's rubbers are tingley??. There was a long pause, and then she said, "Pardon me?" "Are Hosmer's rubbers Tingley (a prominent brand at the time for shoe rubbers)" I re-uttered. "I have noooo idea!" Carol retorted. Then it hit me, and I started laughing. "Galoshes", I said, "galoshes"...she then laughed too.

One other Hosmer story... I remember him telling of a trip he and the late Tom Zaia, and another attorney whose name I will withhold, made to a bar association meeting at the Candlelight restaurant in Parish. On the way, the other attorney stopped talking, and appeared to be asleep. He wasn't asleep. Turns out, he was dead. So Tom Zaia and Hosmer, upon realizing what had happened, pulled to the side of the road to decide what to do, and then they determined the best course of action was to drive to the nearest funeral home in Mexico, and drop off the body, before proceeding on to the bar association meeting. Which they did. There is more to the story, but you get the picture. Neither rain, nor snow, nor dropping dead along the way should ever preclude you attendance at an annual bar association get together!

Hosmer was a great advocate for the Oswego Library, and was the hospital attorney for many years, and a pretty good golfer, as his golfing buddies like the late Clark Morrison, Dave Read, Jim Cullinan, John Conway, and many others could attest. Most of all, he was the living embodiment of what it meant to be a small town lawyer with a devotion to the law, to principle, and to his family and to his church. F. Hosmer Culkin lived long, and prospered. May his life and the legacy he left, continue to be an inspiration to us all.

END

Printed in the United States
By Bookmasters